Beat your goals

Books to make you better

Books to make you better. To make you *be* better, *do* better, *feel* better. Whether you want to upgrade your personal skills or change your job, whether you want to improve your managerial style, become a more powerful communicator, or be stimulated and inspired as you work.

Prentice Hall Business is leading the field with a new breed of skills, careers and development books. Books that are a cut above the mainstream – in topic, content and delivery – with an edge and verve that will make you better, with less effort.

Books that are as sharp and smart as you are.

Prentice Hall Business.
We work harder – so you don't have to.

For more details on products, and to contact us, visit
www.business-minds.com
www.yourmomentum.com

DAVID MOLDEN AND DENISE PARKER

Beat your goals

The definitive guide to personal success

an imprint of Pearson Education

London • New York • Toronto • Sydney • Tokyo • Singapore • Hong Kong • Cape Town

New Delhi • Madrid • Paris • Amsterdam • Munich • Milan • Stockholm

PEARSON EDUCATION LIMITED

Head Office:
Edinburgh Gate
Harlow CM20 2JE
Tel: +44 (0)1279 623623
Fax: +44 (0)1279 431059

London Office:
128 Long Acre
London WC2E 9AN
Tel: +44 (0)20 7447 2000
Fax: +44 (0)20 7240 5771
Website: www.business-minds.com

First published in Great Britain in 2002

The right of David Molden and Denise Parker to be identified as Authors of this Work has been asserted by them in accordance with the Copyright, Designs and Patents Act 1988.

ISBN 0 273 65670 8

British Library Cataloguing in Publication Data
A CIP catalogue record for this book can be obtained from the British Library

10 9 8 7 6 5 4 3 2 1

Designed by Claire Brodmann Book Designs, Lichfield, Staffs
Typeset by Northern Phototypesetting Co. Ltd, Bolton
Printed and bound in Great Britain by Biddles Ltd, Guildford & King's Lynn

The Publishers' policy is to use paper manufactured from sustainable forests.

Contents

Acknowledgements

Thanks and appreciation to all those who supported this goal! May you continue to achieve all that you want in life.

We extend special thanks to the following. All those who asked: 'What makes your book different from all the others?' Friends, too numerous to mention, from whom we continue to learn each and every day. To our talented colleagues and contemporaries, especially Jon Symes, Barbara Allan, Tomas Ruzicka, Tom Tait and Tanesh Bhugobaun. To individuals who have provided special sources of inspiration, including Deepak Chopra, Sanaya Roman, the Dalai Lama and Sikung Michael Tse.

Denise: Thanks to inspirational teachers including Beryl Heather, Liz Newton, Ian Newton, John Overdurf, Julie Silverthorn and Gordon Spence, to Dave, business partner and co-creator of this goal, and to my parents and sister for their love and support. And, of course, to my conscious, my unconscious and my higher consciousness!

David: To all the people who have given me leadership in the theatre of learning we commonly refer to as life. I have drawn inspiration and higher awareness from the most unexpected sources, and the most everyday experiences.

And we both thank Richard Stagg, Rachael Stock and Rachel Russell at Pearson – your insight and enthusiasm for this project have helped us remain focused on our overall outcome of giving maximum benefit and value to our readers around the world.

Introduction

Imagine you're travelling on a boat down a river or across an ocean. It might be a powerboat, a sailing boat or any other kind you choose... If you just let the current carry you along, you might be lucky and reach your desired destination, or more than likely you'll arrive somewhere different that may not be where you want to get to. If, on the other hand, you rely on engine power, plot your journey in detail and steer a straight course, you might find that the currents or winds still take you off course. And if you decide to go up stream or against the current this is likely to be hard work, you'll use more fuel, meet oncoming traffic and encounter resistance. Then again, you might be a passenger on someone else's boat and see interesting sights along the journey yet not get the opportunity to stop and explore the places you'd most like to visit.

Imagine instead letting the current take you in the general direction and, at the same time, making choices about how you steer the boat. This way you get to make adjustments to your journey – maybe you'll take a detour, explore new territory, stop off along the way, get the boat checked out, refuel and choose where you want to go. Occasionally you might encounter obstacles like bad weather or engine trouble and these can be overcome, and valuable lessons learned, when you balance the pull of the current with your own will and actions.

The skipper who ignores the currents and weather conditions will struggle to reach his destination and the skipper who doesn't steer the boat

well will drift out to sea and may never get to where he wants. But the skipper who balances both will enjoy the journey and arrive with the boat intact.

Some people have asked us: 'So what makes your book different from other books on goal setting?'

Some of you, and particularly those who have already achieved many goals in your lives, may well find aspects in this book that seem familiar. And if you do, then we're delighted that you're already doing some of the things that work! But this book is about much more than that. We want you to really Be, Do and Have what you want in business and in life. That's why we've approached this book in a different way from many others.

The tools that we offer are based on practice, not just theory, and are taken from people who have themselves been successful in achieving their goals, from NLP (neuro linguistic programming), the art and science of excellence, and from a blend of Western and Eastern philosophies from Zig Ziglar to the Dalai Lama.

This book isn't just about using your head…it's about using the whole of you because whatever you think you are, you're much more than that!

To begin we encourage you to think differently about your goals by considering the question 'What is a goal?' Is it simply a target to be achieved or is it more of a journey in life? In the early chapters we help you to reflect on your goals and how they fit with who you are, and encourage you to think bigger than ever before.

We then move on to explore what stops some of us from achieving what we want and how some people succeed in achieving goals in some areas of their lives and not in others. Here you will uncover any personal barriers you have and discover powerful tools and strategies for overcoming these.

Once you've cleared away these barriers to success, and not before, you're ready to set your goals. We offer you some creative ways to help you do this so that you can be sure that your goals have real meaning and are truly compelling. Unlike other books, this isn't just about deciding what you want and working hard to make it happen. It's about using different ways of thinking and about using *all* the resources you have – your conscious mind, your unconscious mind and, for those of you who choose to believe, your higher consciousness, too.

And it doesn't end there. Setting your goals is an important stage and what you do next really will determine how successful you are. In Chapter 8 we offer you some tips and strategies for staying on track, beating your goals and becoming a serial high achiever. For those of you who still believe that achievement is just about hard work, you'll find a combination of strategies, some conventional and others less so, some that use a logical left-brain approach and others that utilise your right brain resources too for more effective use of your time and energy.

Last of all, we include a reminder about the importance of learning from your experience and of recognising and celebrating your success!

Throughout the book you will find links to web resources specifically designed to enhance your learning, remove barriers and help you set and achieve your goals. Many of these resources are questionnaires and exercises to provide feedback, raise awareness and keep you on the right track. Like many things in life, the most effective tools are those that are tailor-made for a specific purpose, and this book has been designed to offer each and every reader the flexibility to customise their own pathway to success. In it you will find a wide range of tools and ideas you can use to coach yourself to becoming a high achiever.

So, if you have goals that you haven't yet brought to life, or if you have already achieved great things in some areas of your life but not in others, we invite you to use this book as a personal resource from

which to draw ideas, strategies and practical techniques. Take what works best for you and have fun as you 'beat your goals'.

We look forward to hearing all your success stories.

CHAPTER 1

What is your goal?

You will no doubt have set yourself a goal at some point in your life, and may even have two, three or more on the go at any one time. Goals are built on desires – the things we want in life – and the stronger the desire, the more energy we put into achieving it. Yet a desire on its own is not a goal.

People talk a great deal about achieving *goals* and creating *dreams* for the future. How many, though, actually use their goals to achieve their dreams? It is easy to confuse the two, yet it isn't so easy to succeed with a goal that is unattached to a dream or vision. You really need them both. And this is not all you will require if you want to consistently beat your goals.

"Reach high, for stars lie hidden in your soul. Dream deep, for every dream precedes the goal."
                                                                    Pamela Vaull Starr

Have you ever spent time dreaming about something you would like to have, perhaps a tropical island holiday, a house in the country, or a new job with improved pay and conditions, and then done nothing about getting it? That is a dream, and it may or may not contain desire. Desire arouses the motivation to get up and do something, while dreams may only act on us in the moment, providing a brief respite from the realities of the day. It's the combination of these three elements – *dreams, desires and goals* – that provides the conditions to succeed.

The dream creates an image of a future that you find motivating, and this builds desire. The goals you put in place will help you to realise your dream by focusing your attention on each step of the journey.

Harnessing dreams and desires of the heart

"The future belongs to those who believe in the beauty of their dreams.**"**

Eleanor Roosevelt

The mind is a wonderful thing, with such enormous creative potential, bound only by our limiting thoughts of what we believe is and isn't possible in the world. Dreams free the mind from the physical world and engage the heart to conjure images of possibilities. This is an amazing ability, tapping into a deep intelligence, or higher consciousness, closer to intuition and spirit than to anything physically measurable.

When you engage inner wisdom in this way, you unleash an energy that believes anything is possible. If you use your analytical mind too much you might limit your ability to dream freely and become trapped in a world full of detail, complexity, sequence, logic and limitation. Some people are unfamiliar with this deeper intelligence because the analytical mind is more used to focusing on the physical world. A mind that has been highly trained to analyse and accumulate facts may block the ability to access creative imagination or work with it for any length of time.

Whether you consciously think about goal setting or not, the things you do and say are influenced by your dreams and your desires. Whatever you spend time thinking about you will seek to bring into being, often unconsciously. How many times have you dreamily thought about something and soon after found yourself connected with that something?

Tomas, a professional tennis coach, invited us to Wimbledon tennis championships to coach one of the top men's doubles players who wanted some help to remain in a confident state of mind and 'in the flow' even when down on points. We were talking about this and imagining how we might do more work with top sports professionals. A few days later, on a flight to Lisbon, Denise just happened to be seated next to a top 200m runner and ended up coaching him to be more resourceful on the track.

Some people call it synchronicity, others manifestation. The more we talk with people about these experiences (and we have so many like this), the more we hear similar stories from other people. When you try to analyse what's happening there are no concrete conclusions, and so we have learned to accept that there is a deeper intelligence or energy of some kind working that we are not yet able to analyse, and we are happy to go with it and just enjoy the results.

Whatever is causing these unexpected encounters is coming more from the imagination than from logic and planning. So, if you have a natural ability to attract the things you want or to create the opportunity to get the things you want, why not learn how to use this ability and maximise the potential for turning your dreams and desires into reality? This is where goal setting comes in. A great deal of goal setting happens without dreams and without desire. Some of our clients tell us of all the things they must achieve that stress them out. When there is desire within, there is no stress. Instead you have an inner drive, a positive urge to succeed, and the motivation to overcome obstacles along the way – and this leaves you feeling good. Stress can create ill health and is prevalent when your thoughts are consumed with worry about what you want to get rid of or avoid. This state often results from being engaged in goals that have little or no personal meaning for you. If you

> **So when your dreams, desire and goal setting are integrated and working in unison, you have all the key ingredients for realising the things in life that you really want**

have ever been a slave to another person's goal in this way, you may recall having had little or no desire to see it succeed.

So when your dreams, desire and goal setting are integrated and working in unison, you have all the key ingredients for realising the things in life that you really want – the things that up until now you may only have dreamed about – and you will be well on the way to beating your goals.

> "Vision without a task is only a dream. A task without a vision is but drudgery. But vision with a task is a dream fulfilled." Willie Stone

What do you want to achieve?

We are frequently surprised at the kinds of things people tell us they want to achieve. Here are just a few that we have come across in the past month or so.

- To complete the Santiago trail on foot.
- To become an independent business consultant.
- To become a top business coach.
- To get a job working with special needs children.
- To become financially independent by the age of 40.
- To start a family.
- To work in a different country.
- To learn a foreign language.

- To live a healthier lifestyle.

- To grow a business to $1 million in nine months.

- To stop smoking.

- To be more sensitive to and accepting of other people's needs.

Almost anything can constitute a goal, and for now it's sufficient to make sure that your goal is something that you want, is future oriented, and that there is some form of measurement so that you know when you have achieved it. A more complete framework for goal setting is covered elsewhere in the book.

Here are some contexts to help you think about the kind of goals you might like to pursue. As you scan the list you may do so dreamily, and sense when there is desire in your heart, a good feeling or real motivation. You might want to make a quick evaluation of how satisfied you are in your life right now, with each of the categories in the list. Score on a scale of 1–10 where 1 is very dissatisfied and 10 is extremely satisfied. As this is not an exclusive list, please add your own categories and score in the same way.

EXERCISE	How satisfied are you with your life?

Category	Degree of satisfaction
Financial security	1 -------------- 5 -------------- 10
Personal growth	1 -------------- 5 -------------- 10
Physical health	1 -------------- 5 -------------- 10
Diet	1 -------------- 5 -------------- 10
Material possessions	1 -------------- 5 -------------- 10
Emotional balance	1 -------------- 5 -------------- 10
Career	1 -------------- 5 -------------- 10 ▶

▶ Knowledge   1 -------------- 5 -------------- 10

  Acquiring new skills   1 -------------- 5 -------------- 10

  Being influential   1 -------------- 5 -------------- 10

  Relationships   1 -------------- 5 -------------- 10

  Social life   1 -------------- 5 -------------- 10

  Spirituality   1 -------------- 5 -------------- 10

  Playing a sport   1 -------------- 5 -------------- 10

  Other   1 -------------- 5 -------------- 10

  Other   1 -------------- 5 -------------- 10

How did you get on with this? It is a particularly useful exercise if you do not know what you want, or if you have never evaluated these aspects of your life before. We have met people who as children were so finely groomed and led by their parents, that they have very little desire of their own as adults. They have gone to the school and university and pursued the career chosen by their parents. Other people seem to drift in and out of situations that confront them, doing whatever takes their fancy at any moment, with little thought to what the new situation will bring them. They are enticed by the immediacy of the attraction.

James is an interior designer with a growing list of wealthy clients. He recalls his high school years where he was encouraged to learn a trade that would provide him with a secure future. It didn't matter to his parents, or to his teachers, whether he enjoyed the chosen trade, it was more important to select something with long-term security. So he chose to be an electrical engineer, and while he managed to get along surviving an electric shock now and then, his heart was never really in it. After some meandering around trying this and that, James eventually discovered something completely different that would feed the desire in his heart for many years to come. And so today he can dream about designing interiors that connect with that desire, and he can create goals which engage him in activities that feed the desire and give his life a real sense of purpose.

You may know exactly what you want and be eager to read ahead and begin taking the first steps to making it happen, or you may still be a little unsure about what to put your energy into. Either way, it's worth taking some time now to be sure of what you really want.

When there is a lack of desire, for whatever reason, one way to create it is to review all the occasions when you have been really enjoying yourself and look for common links among the various experiences. Then imagine what kind of goals might engage you in similar activities.

EXERCISE Identifying the enjoyment factor

Take some time to identify those occasions in your life where you have really enjoyed yourself and been full of desire, and plot these events as illustrated below. The process of showing the 'enjoyment factor' in this graphical way provides a strong visible perspective with which to consider the overall impact on your life. Think about the enjoyment factor first before working out what was creating the enjoyment. You will probably have a range in which some things were more enjoyable than others. When you have done this, label each event, then look for patterns linking them (see diagram below). Are there any common features? What is it about each one that is providing the enjoyment? Begin to think how you can recreate these enjoyable experiences more often in the future.

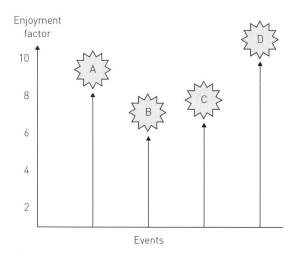

Event	Feature
A	Making important decisions; working with fun people; earning big bucks; having lots of autonomy.
B	Foreign travel; complex project; great team; clear aims.
C	Highly skilled and fun people to work with; flexible working day; great city to visit, especially nightlife.
D	Lots of responsibility; great supportive team; fantastic place to work.

Sometimes the reason why someone may not know what they want is that there are so many things going on in their life that attempts at logical analysis result in divergent directions of thought, stress and tiredness. It may be that the task of deciding which goal to go for is so overwhelming that procrastination takes root and apathy rules. If this is you, it is time to give your thinking mind a rest and hand over the decision making to your heart and your unconscious mind. Relaxation

techniques such as meditation and abdominal breathing will help you slow down your conscious thought processes and engage your deeper intuitive resources. And when you learn to trust your intuition you will begin to find life's most important decisions are easier to make.

Relying exclusively on logical analysis may mean that your life is extremely practical and ordered; however, you may become disconnected from true sensory experience and lose the buzz and zest that bursts out from inner desire. Try this exercise to help choose the life category your heart wants you to work with.

EXERCISE   **Connecting with the heart before engaging the mind**

Find a quiet place and sit comfortably on a hard chair with your back straight and unsupported, and your feet flat on the floor. Rest your hands palm down on your knees and relax. Start at the top of the head and move all the way down your body relaxing each part of your body. Make sure you include your jaw, shoulders, fingers and toes, as these are common places where stress causes problems. Breathe deeply and softly through your nose. Take the air down to your abdomen as you allow all tension to fall away so that you are totally relaxed. If any thoughts come into your mind, just allow them to float through you and away into the atmosphere.

Now you are fully relaxed, concentrate on one life category at a time. For each one, say the name and put your attention to your heart. Resist the mind's urge to have thoughts that are related to the life category. Close down the analytical mind for a short time and hand control over to the heart. Just connect your mind with your heart and sense how you feel. Your unconscious will tell you which life category is most important for you to develop. You may get a sensation or experience a strong sense of trusting yourself to know which part of your life to focus on.

 It may be that the task of deciding which goal to go for is so overwhelming that procrastination takes root and apathy rules.

Some of you may be very clear about what you want, and this might not be contained in just one goal or desire but in many. In this situation it is more a question of determining which goal is the most important and looking at common needs that may be served by each goal. We will cover this scenario in Chapter 5, with appropriate exercises to help you work out your personal values and priorities. At this stage the emphasis is on making a distinction between a) pseudo-desires generated by the analytical mind, either in response to being influenced by other people or as a result of habitual thinking patterns, and b) true desires of the heart that create inner visceral feelings when imagining the journey towards the dream. Goals are more likely to be achieved when they are connected to both a desire and a dream. The dream is what you want, the desire is how you feel about wanting it, and the goal is a pragmatic 'how to' sequence of steps for achieving it.

The power of imagination

"I am enough of an artist to draw freely upon my imagination. Imagination is more important than knowledge. Knowledge is limited. Imagination encircles the world ... When I examine myself and my methods of thought, I come to the conclusion that the gift of fantasy has meant more to me than my talent for absorbing positive knowledge." Albert Einstein

Think about an apple. Make it a red, crisp, shiny apple. Imagine someone taking a bite from that apple and hear the crunching of the teeth. Is that a clear picture? You can use the same process to visualise a goal. The mind can work with two types of thought – either it will utilise existing knowledge or it will imagine something from outside the realm of knowledge. Very often the two get so intertwined that they become mixed up, imagination being frequently mistaken for knowledge. Have you ever been in a creative thinking situation where someone has said 'that will never work'? This statement relates to the future and therefore the mind must be working with imagination, but it is contaminated with knowledge, because to say 'that will never work' you have to be referring to past experience. Knowledge relates to the past, and when we attempt to project what we know into the future as a process of imagination, we limit our potential and creative ability. Our thoughts then become contained within a restricted and contaminated reality. Pure imagination has no boundaries or constraints. It is free like the wind.

The mind's ability to imagine the future is extremely powerful if you allow it to be free from knowledge. Knowledge is useful when you want to analyse a situation or form a conclusion about something. Imagination is not an analytical process; it has no borders, conditions, presumptions, time limits or evaluative criteria. It is free, flowing, unfettered, abundant and wild. When imagination is based on knowledge it is not pure imagination. There is a time for imagination and a time for analysis and evaluation. A mixture of the two in the same thinking process can be a very dangerous cocktail.

Fuzzy and clear goals

Your goals may be small, or large; the size will depend upon many different factors and this is one aspect of life where size really doesn't matter, as long as it is connected to a dream and it creates a feeling of desire. Likewise, some goals are clear and others fuzzy, and this does make a difference. Have a go at imagining a goal now. Create a visual in your mind of having achieved the goal. Put the book down for a few moments and work on the mental image.

Done that? What is your image like? Does it contain detail or is it fuzzy and more general in appearance? There is no right or wrong way to visualise, it is more appropriate to ask 'what do I want?' and design the image around the answer to that question. The more specific, clear and detailed the image, the more likely it is that you will get exactly what it contains. It is less likely that you will discover other attractive options as you pursue your goal. So, be careful what you imagine because you will probably get it. We meet so many people in business with a habit of visualising negative situations they want to avoid, and they tell us how awful their job or their life has become. Their life has not become awful; they have created it for themselves! If you have this tendency – and it is not uncommon – stay with us and you'll learn some techniques to help you change the way you think and influence your future.

"Goals too clearly defined can become blinkers." Mary Catherine Bateson

A more general mental image with very little detail will open the way to other possibilities being presented to you. It will also bring things that you might not have considered and these may or may not be welcome surprises. The choice here usually comes down to a mix of two things: 1) the way you respond to unexpected situations, and 2) how determined you are to get exactly what you want.

Example

Let's say you have a goal to get a well-paid job in a country with a warm climate. This would be enough detail for a fuzzy goal, and you might imagine yourself sitting in an office looking out of an open window at your luxury car gleaming in the sunshine. The car is no specific make or model. A more detailed goal would include the exact country and region, the type of work you will be doing, and something to suggest how much money you are earning. Now, you may not really have considered the type of work you want to do, and this missing detail may make decisions more stressful as you are presented with job offers you had not anticipated or included as a possibility.

So, as you are dreaming your 'goal image', make distinctions between what you really want to get and what you are happy to leave open to chance and opportunity. In that way you can build in the things you desire most and leave some room for other options that might appear.

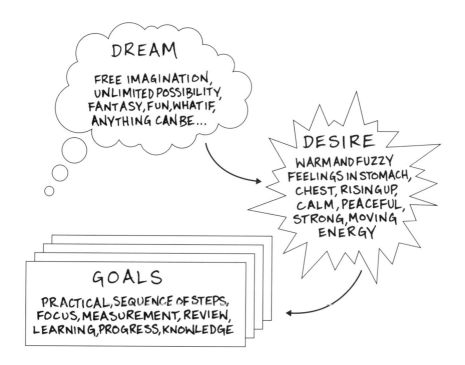

The goal and the journey

"It is good to have an end to journey toward; but it is the journey that matters, in the end."

Ursula K. LeGuin

You may have heard the story about a man who spent most of his life in pursuit of money and material gain. He was very clear about what he wanted and how he was going to get it. So fixed was his mind on the goal that he often seemed distant in business meetings and with his family. His mind was almost constantly in planning mode, working out the next steps to his goal, which he achieved after many years of hard

work and long hours away from home. He acquired great wealth, invested in property and bought stock in some highly successful companies. This goal was so important to him that it overshadowed everything else in his life, including his family and his health. His children left home and never contacted him, his marriage broke down acrimoniously, and he suffered many health problems, including back trouble, shortness of breath, high blood pressure and severe migraine. His family disowned him and none of his work associates visited him in hospital when he was having a triple bypass heart operation. He died a lonely man.

This very sad tale has an important and very human message for us all. When making goals, remember that the journey to the goal is your life in the present moment, and your life is made up of one moment followed by the next and the next and so on. Enjoy your life today, because if you cannot enjoy today you may not know how to enjoy tomorrow, or the next day, or the day when you do eventually achieve your goal. Don't get tricked into thinking that when you have achieved your goal and you have your house, car, business, new body, job or whatever, you will be happy and content. Happiness is a state of mind, and if you cannot find a way of being happy today, any feelings of happiness you get from achieving your goal may be short-lived.

Happiness comes from within and is self-generated. If the purpose of your goal is to make you happy, then how happy are you now? Unhappy people spend most of their time in varying degrees of emotional states such as sadness or anger, actually creating mental blocks to happiness, and as a consequence of this they pay very little attention to goals. When you are happy, the goals you achieve will make life richer and

Happiness is a state of mind, and if you cannot find a way of being happy today, any feelings of happiness you get from achieving your goal may be short-lived.

more rewarding for you, and the happiness will still come from within, from your heart and from your spirit.

When you are following a path that fits you like a glove – and you will instinctively know the path that fits best for you – your happiness can grow even stronger. Is the path you are on today the best fit for you?

❝When we are motivated by goals that have deep meaning, by dreams that need completion, by pure love that needs expressing, then we truly live life.❞
Greg Anderson

What's your outcome?

Once there were three stonecutters who were asked by a passer-by why they were cutting stone. The first one replied: 'I'm just cutting stones, can't you see?' The second replied: 'I'm earning a living for my family.' The third replied with a smile: 'I'm building a magnificent cathedral.'

Sometimes you don't always get what you want. You may get some of what you want, and some things you hadn't bargained for. That often happens when you focus on a goal alone. Or you may get what you want and miss some terrific opportunities by being too narrowly focused.

> Shirley runs a small business and wants to make it into the big time. She organised some promotional events, which were very successful in the local area where she operates her business. She has not yet made the big time, but she has made an impact in the local community. She is very talented and has good business acumen with excellent people skills. So, what is keeping Shirley from making the big time? Perhaps it's the focus on the goal and not on the outcome.

By focusing on the *outcome* of a goal you can think bigger and wider than the goal itself and bring the purpose to bear on the results.

> If Shirley were to consider the purpose of the promotions and think about the outcomes she wants from the work required to organise, plan and prepare for each event, her thinking might be extended to accommodate her dream of making the big time and perhaps she might just begin to touch the reality of her dream.

Some companies today confuse targets, goals and outcomes. An outcome includes all the consequences of pursuing any specific goal or set of goals. It pays always to have an outcome in mind when defining a goal.

> Vanessa's manager set her a target of making 30 sales calls per day. Achievable perhaps, but questionable as to its effect on the business goal of increasing sales by 15 per cent. It is a service company, and the route to growing sales in any service business is quality of service, relationship with clients and referrals to prospects. Quick, cold sales calls may notch up points on a daily target list but are unlikely to increase sales significantly over the long term.

A recent news article refers to 'targets in the UK's National Health Service aimed at reducing the size of patient waiting lists'. The article reports how these targets are having an adverse effect on patient care because doctors and surgeons are picking the easiest cases with the simplest procedures. This is the quickest way of reducing the waiting list. The consequence is that more complicated and sophisticated treatments are getting relegated to the bottom of the list. The target actually serves as a block to achieving the overall aim of improving the quality of healthcare.

It seems that some leaders have learned nothing from the quality guru W. Edwards Deming who, 50 years ago, said: 'If you give people targets and make their careers dependent on delivering them, they will likely meet the targets, even if they have to destroy the enterprise to do it.'

If you manage by target setting, then think through all the consequences to check you are contributing to the higher purpose. You can quickly check by asking yourself:

- What outcomes do I want to get from this activity?
- How will I know if the activity is achieving the outcomes?

When you are working to a target, what is the measure of quality applied to the process? If the goal is to achieve a number, what does that number represent? Is it OK to have 50 new customers if the majority have been persuaded to buy from you against their better judgement? All these questions reinforce the importance of the journey and the overall outcome that the goal, and all its sub-goals, are designed to achieve.

Remember, it's not where you arrive at that matters most, it's the path you travel and the methods deployed to get there that develop strength, wisdom and intelligence, and ultimately determine your outcomes.

Additional resources are available from the authors' website — **Quadrant1.com.**
Go to **www.quadrant1.com**, click on know-how and select the title you want.

▶ Garden of riches

▶ Life balance

▶ Happiness.

CHAPTER

2

Chariot of dreams

> "The vision of something new and a belief so strong that it becomes a reality."
> Anita Roddick on the qualities needed to become a natural entrepreneur

If you have seen the film archive of Martin Luther King where he uttered the famous words 'I have a dream', you will recall how he seemed to be in his dream as he was saying it. The tone of voice and body language express the desire to live the dream, and perhaps this offered people a sense of what their future lives could become. This is pure inspiration. A human connection linking one heart to the hearts of others.

The inauguration speech of Nelson Mandela was similarly inspirational, driven by a deep desire for a future South Africa where all races and creeds would live together. Wherever you can observe motivational speeches like these you will find the same ingredients – a dream for the future with a strong desire bringing it to life in the present. And it's not only leaders such as these that have dreams and desires. A close friend had a dream and a strong desire to radically change her career and it took her only six months to achieve it!

The key message in all these examples is that often a goal or a dream alone is not enough. As we said in the previous chapter, creating the desire to go with these will give you the biggest chance of success. In this chapter you will discover more about how to cultivate a deep desire, like harnessing a team of horses to the chariot of your dreams.

Dreaming the dream

Dreams are like carefully constructed works of art and when we experience a vivid dream it can be like watching a film where we get carried away by storylines of endless possibilities. Dreaming is something we all do using our unconscious resources (although some people remember dreams more easily than others) and can happen when we are sleeping or when we are awake. The French talk about 'making' a dream rather than 'having' a dream and this is probably a more accurate description since we each have the ability to let our minds wander and create all manner of scenarios. You may daydream while awake about a future holiday, an adventure, winning a sporting competition, building a successful business or any other goals and desires. You may already be in pursuit of a dream or you may have more than one dream to follow. Whatever stage you are at with your dreams, there are some practical techniques you can use to give them more impact and help beat your goals.

When you relax, dreaming comes easily. Just close your eyes and imagine something – anything! Can you picture sitting on a white horse and riding off into the sunset? That's the imagination at play.

So what is your dream for the future? What journey is worth spending time on so that you get the best possible results? Choose one and we'll get started. When you are working with your imagination, there are no rules, only ideas, choices and a blank canvas. So, before you begin to think about your dream, think about play. On what occasions have you been most playful in your life? Where do you go to play? Where could

> **When good things happen, your thoughts will be bright and beneficial to your state of mind. When bad things happen, your thoughts may be less positive in how they affect you.**

you go to get into a playful state of mind? For some people it may be at the top of a hill or mountain. Others may prefer a coastal location. How about a kindergarten? Young children have lots of playful energy to draw from. Your playful location may be somewhere like a quiet garden, or by the bank of a river. Choose somewhere that helps you to draw on the playful aspect of your imagination, and remember to enjoy yourself during this process. Any stress can float away down the river or fade into the sky as you relax your body and mind into the state of playful dreaming. You may want to do this alone, or if other people will be riding with you in your chariot, play together and create a dream that you can all engage with.

Be the artist of your dreams

There are two Buddhist sayings, 'what you think you create' and 'you are the result of all your thinking'. If you live from day to day with little idea of what you want to become, your thoughts will define themselves from your experience. When good things happen, your thoughts will be bright and beneficial to your state of mind. When bad things happen, your thoughts may be less positive in how they affect you. If you are happy leaving your future to chance, then living day to day will facilitate this. If you would rather have an influence on the shape of your future, using your imagination is highly recommended.

| EXERCISE | Intuitive imagination |

You may begin with a review of your experience and focus on the times when you have enjoyed yourself and on the range of skills you have acquired. Acknowledge these things, then clear the canvas and prepare for the future. As you are entering into a playful mood notice any images that appear in your mind, and allow them to take whatever form they want. The general nature of the images will be determined by your deep intuitive intelligence, creating a canvas where your future will be painted.

You now become the artist with a set of brushes and a palette of strong primary colours. Imagine enriching your image with bright colours and adding whatever details come to mind. The amount of detail is less important than the quality of the image, as this is what will give it impact. As you change the qualities, be sensitive to your internal feelings and notice which quality creates the feeling of desire. For some people this may be richness of colour, for others the size or location of the image will make the difference, or perhaps changing from a two-dimensional image to 3D will intensify the desire.

As you are building up the picture you may notice sounds emerging. As an artist you can work with these also, as if you have a sound-mixing desk to alter the volume, bass, treble, stereo effect, depth, vibrato, chorus, delay and any other qualities that make the overall experience more vivid and real. Notice how that initial thought is now becoming a multi-media experience, and this is exactly what you are creating – an experience that you are going to have in the future, and a desire that brings good feelings as you journey from where you are now to where you want to be.

This inner experience may also be surreal or symbolic in form. The image does not have to resemble anything particular and the sounds do not have to make sense. As long as the completed inner experience harnesses a desire, which might be a feeling in the abdomen, rising up through the chest and neck to make the mouth smile and the eyes sparkle, it's working. You might check the intensity of this feeling by playing with the different qualities of the image and sounds, and noticing if the feeling gets weaker or stronger. There is a direct link, and when you find the one critical quality that has this immediate effect on your feelings, you can use that quality any time you want to reconnect with your dream.

Here are the words of Tenley Albright, M.D., Olympic Gold Medal Figure Skater, who at the age of 11 was suddenly stricken with poliomyelitis and was confined to her bed, unable to walk. As she

recovered the use of her legs, she took up skating again and, only four months later, won the Eastern United States Junior Ladies Figure Skating competition.

> One Monday morning, the doctors came in and said to me, 'On Friday we are going to ask you to take three steps.' That was the first time I ever remember visualising. Looking back now, I didn't realise it then. I worked all week, lying on my bed, thinking what it would be like and how I would somehow manage to take three steps. Friday morning came and somehow I did manage. And that was really the start of my recovery.[1]

Practise dreaming creatively to find ways that work best for you and use the additional tips that follow for even greater impact.

Storyboarding

You may find that one image does not fully represent your dream, while a story with a sequence of images, or a play with different scenes, is more appropriate for you. These might be arranged along a horizontal or vertical plane or in some other formation that seems to fit for you. If you use a storyboard effect the images are more likely to be in frames, unless you have some method of superimposing images in the same location. Images with frames are more likely to contain specific detail as it suggests that your dream is exclusive and only the things inside the frame will be considered when constructing goals. Images without frames may be open to the influence of your ongoing experience, which will appeal to people who want to keep their options open in case something really juicy comes their way. Have a go at this simple exercise to discover what difference it makes for you.

---

1 Reprinted from **www.achievement.org** with permission from the American Academy of Achievement.

EXERCISE	The effect of using frames

First put your inner experience into a frame, then remove the frame and imagine the image, and any sounds, filling the entire canvas of your mind. Notice how it can extend in all directions and fade into the distance. Which one appeals to you the most? Framed or unframed?

Physiology of dreaming

There are ways of positioning the body and the eyes to aid the art of dreaming. It doesn't matter whether you are standing, sitting or lying flat out on the sofa, it's the head and eyes that are important. If the neck is bent so that the head and eyes are looking down, relative to the position of the spine, you may struggle to create rich, colourful images. In this position inner dialogue is encouraged which may interfere with the dreaming process. You are more likely to find it easier with your head slightly up and eyes also up – just above the horizontal is fine. Play around with this until you find a position that works best for you. Start by looking down at the floor or at the bottom of a wall and try creating an image in your mind of a future experience. Next, move your head up and gaze out of a window and do the same. Notice the difference this makes for you. Remember to relax your body and breathing, and especially your mind.

David was at Wimbledon this year talking with Petr Pala, ranked 14th in the world in men's tennis doubles. As they were discussing the difference between a good and bad day on the court he noticed that Pala's head was up when thinking about the good days and down when thinking about the bad days. When his head was down he was also telling himself how badly he was playing and reinforcing a lower standard of play. When his head was up the internal dialogue stopped and his entire body became lighter and more flexible. Petr and his partner Pavel made it to the quarter-finals on that occasion and played an epic game lasting four-and-a-half hours on a sweltering mid-summer day.

How much do you want it?

There's a difference between having a desire for something and wanting something so much that it begins to create unhealthy levels of stress. Some stress is useful. We have coping mechanisms for dealing with it and it can spur us on to make things happen. But when stress gets above a certain level – and this will be different for each of us – the coping mechanism is overpowered. This can then result in psychological imbalance and physical damage to internal organs, joints and circulation. Also, the immune system becomes less effective at fighting infection.

If you do experience an unhealthy build-up inside, practise relaxing and smiling inwardly, knowing that the future will turn out as you want it to, without having to strive too much. Let go of any tension you feel with the desire, allow the feeling to become relaxed and warm, with a regular rhythm like waves falling on the shore.

If you find yourself using negative words such as 'if I don't achieve this dream I don't know what I will do', you are not relaxed. Too strong a

> **Too strong a wanting has a tendency to consume your life and create unhappiness.**

wanting has a tendency to consume your life and create unhappiness. Remind yourself that the journey in pursuit of your dream is going to be something really special. Find a way of desiring and letting go at the same time. Having a belief and determination is different from being intensely driven by a fear of what might happen if success evades you.

Courage

"You can make any dream come true – all you need is courage."

Walt Disney

Some dreams may seem so far-fetched as to appear scary. Just the thought of them may create uncertainty and doubt. Dreams can stretch your inner resources and move you to a higher level of being, when you are able to muster enough courage to take the first steps, and when you have strategies for dealing with uncertainty and doubt. A dream with no stretch factor is unlikely to create a strong desire. Here's what the philosopher Peter Geach had to say about courage:

"A virtue indispensable to the good life: a readiness to persist in a valued project, despite risk of harm, injury, death, censure or loss of personal standing. Given the nature of the human life-world, few worthwhile enterprises are possible for those who will take no avoidable risks: such a policy would entail (at the everyday level) no parenthood, little travel, few ventures in work or play; and (in extreme situations) no standing up to tyranny, no speaking out against injustice. For an act to be courageous, as distinct from reckless, or stubborn, or obstinate, the risks must be reasonable in relation to the goal, and the goal itself soundly appraised." From *The Virtues*, Peter Geach, Cambridge Press, 1977

Dreams that move you outside your comfort zone will stretch you, and the more stretch goals you achieve, the more your confidence will grow and the bigger the stretches may become. Someone said recently that the best business goals are big, hairy and audacious because for them this means the goal is a sufficient stretch to create a desire that whilst a little scary is balanced with inner confidence. So courage is an important ingredient that will be tested only in action, and in later chapters you will learn how to prepare the path by removing uncertainty and doubt.

Meditate on your dream

Many people nowadays meditate to prevent the pressure in their work from turning to stress, for balancing energy and for relaxation. Slouching in front of the TV is not the same thing. Proper relaxation has a purpose. Hobbies such as fishing, painting, reading and golf are relaxing, as are more physical activities such as rock climbing and martial arts. Any activity that is enjoyable, proactive, has a clear and simple purpose and which focuses the mind on simple things will be relaxing. Watching TV is a passive act, with lots of changing visual stimuli, and is more likely to add to stress than reduce it. You can have more fun inside your own mind visualising your dreams and goals and generating desire. TV will not do this for you.

Why not spend a few minutes of quiet time meditating or focusing on your canvas, your dream? The more often you bring it into your mind, the greater impact it will have on your desire and your behaviour – and what you focus on is often what you get. You can do this with your eyes open or closed. Have a go at both and see which you find easiest. When you have completed your canvas of future experience why not bring it into your mind as you are going to sleep and let your unconscious dreaming state go to work on it?

Inner resources

Your dreams, desires and goals will require fuel to provide the energy you will need to pursue and achieve them. Some of this fuel may come from external means, such as other people, your bank account, or perhaps someone else's bank account! The degree by which you are able to muster support for your goals will depend upon your ability to utilise your internal resources. So an awareness of the various resources available, and the connection between inner and outer resources, are vital ingredients in the 'beat your goals' formula. One of the key elements in the achievement of any goal is the ability to influence others in such a way that it is their choice to help you, and this can only come from within – your internal resources.

Having access to external resources is no guarantee of success. Achievement does not necessarily favour those with financial means or external support, but rather those with access to inner resources such as determination, self-belief, positive outlook and creative thinking, to name just a handful.

In 1961, Viv Nicholson won £150,000 on the UK football pools – big money in those days. After winning that money Viv's life became increasingly problematic and emotionally devastating, and the money just added to her troubles. She clearly did not have the inner resources to make the most of her riches and very quickly squandered them away on a lavish and extravagant lifestyle.

Some people have plenty of money and yet their methods of generating wealth seem to create further problems and stress in their life. Others spend their lives losing and regaining their wealth. When your inner resources are aligned for success, the assets you accumulate are a small part of the success equation.

"A man is a success if he gets up in the morning and gets to bed at night, and in between he does what he wants to do."   Bob Dylan

How we measure success is different for each of us and depends on the criteria we choose to measure against. These might include money, happiness, relationships, achievement, career, health or whatever else is important. Ultimately, it is a product of the mind and how you choose to live your life.

It seems that no matter how well off you are in the material sense, true wealth is more about the ability to develop and utilise your inner resources, of which there are many for you to draw from. In this chapter we look at some inner resources that are common among consistently successful people, how people block access to these resources, and ways to remove these blocks.

Knowledge and experience

As we go through life we accumulate knowledge and experience and use this growing store as a reference for future decisions. Herein lie both a comfort and a danger. If you base all goal decisions on the contents of this store you may merely be extending your capability by small steps, and this may give you a high success rate at achieving small things. Very comfortable, and fine if that's what you want. On the other hand, if you would rather take bigger steps and achieve greater things, your store of knowledge and experience may not contain all that you need to consistently beat your goals.

The degree by which your store of knowledge and experience will support your goals comes down to context. For example, if you work in a bank and your goal is to get promoted from counter clerk to loans adviser, you may require only a little more knowledge about that particular function. However, if your goal is to set up your own business and supply services to banks, unless you are already in that business you will require a great deal more knowledge to help you in the very different context of business owner and service provider. You will probably want to tap into the experiences of others who are working in the same business. Sometimes the knowledge we have can be a barrier to success where the context is very different. You may experience this just a little when you try to do something in a foreign country for the first time that you normally do at home without having to think very much, like driving on the other side of the road, for instance.

Sometimes it is useful to unlearn old habits before you can learn new ones, and the amount of new knowledge and experience required to

The degree by which your store of knowledge and experience will support your goals comes down to context.

support a goal is somewhat proportional to the contextual stretch of the chosen goal. So, whatever your goal is, the journey of achieving it should include the acquisition of new knowledge and new experiences, and even if you think you know it all, other people are finding newer and smarter ways of achieving similar goals to you, so doesn't it make sense to be on the lookout for smarter ways also?

Skill

The same understanding with regard to the context for knowledge and experience applies increasingly to skill, given that many technical skills can become redundant in quite short periods of time as technology and methodology develop and change. It is no longer safe to depend on the skills you learned in your youth, many of which have a limited useful life. The acquisition of new skills, for a growing number of high achievers, is today an accepted part of the ongoing journey of ambition. So, no matter what level of skill you think you have for any particular challenge, a review and assessment of your skills is always a healthy and smart thing to undertake. If you decide that you can beat your goals without learning new skills, how much of a challenge have you really set yourself? The world today is changing so fast that only a fool will get by on assumptions and perceptions of how things are and the limited skills acquired as a young adult. The smart people are continually acquiring new knowledge, experiences and skills.

Mindset

"The outer conditions of a person's life will always be found to reflect their inner beliefs" James Lane Allen

Now we're getting to a vital component of success. Let's begin with a Zen parable.

After winning several archery contests, the young and rather boastful champion challenged a Zen master who was renowned for his skill as an archer. The young man demonstrated remarkable technical proficiency when he hit a distant bull's eye on his first try, and then split that arrow with his second shot. 'There,' he said to the old man, 'see if you can match that!' Undisturbed, the master did not draw his bow but rather motioned for the young archer to follow him up the mountain. Curious about the old fellow's intentions, the champion followed him high into the mountain until they reached a deep chasm spanned by a rather flimsy and shaky log. Calmly stepping out onto the middle of the unsteady and certainly perilous bridge, the old master picked a faraway tree as a target, drew his bow and fired a clean, direct hit. 'Now it is your turn,' he said as he gracefully stepped back onto the safe ground. Staring with terror into the seemingly bottomless and beckoning abyss, the young man could not force himself to step out onto the log, far less shoot at a target. 'You have much skill with your bow,' the master said, sensing his challenger's predicament, 'but you have little skill with the mind that lets loose the shot.'

Creating a winning mindset is a skill you can learn. It can make all the difference to you and the achievement of your goals, so it's worth investing the time to develop and maintain a mindset that will help you succeed. Think of it as a regular part of your health routine and make sure you work on your mindset as often as you shower. You alone are responsible for your mindset and what it gets for you. It drives just about everything you do. It determines how you feel, affects how others perceive you, and creates your level of enthusiasm, depth of focus, determination, willpower and self-discipline, to mention just a few vital resources you will need to access if you are really serious about beating your goals.

EXERCISE Create a goal-beating mindset

Here's a simple exercise you can do to begin working on the mindset that is going to move you closer to beating your goals. First of all let's consider a few vital qualities:

- positive orientation to life
- curiosity to understand
- confidence
- self-belief.

Whatever you want to achieve you need good-sized portions of these four key qualities in the overall make-up of your mindset. Create a short routine of about ten minutes that you can go through each morning, ideally as part of a sitting meditation. There are four simple steps to this routine.

Step 1 Positive orientation

Think only of positives. If anything negative enters your mind, ask the questions, 'what do I want instead of this negative that will help me to beat my goals?' and 'how will I be different without this thought?' Allow any negative thoughts to float away and disappear. Focus on two or three positive experiences you will have that day. If there is a block here, work on building something positive into your day and make each day valuable to you in some way.

Step 2 Curiosity

Next, let your mind move on to something you want to understand more about. Adopt a curious state of mind that enjoys the challenge of discovery. Ask a couple of questions about the thing you want to understand without feeling that you must have the answer now. All the things you need to know will come to you much more easily when you are relaxed.

Step 3 Confidence

Now move your mind onto a future task and create a colourful mind-image of you performing that task with aplomb. See yourself with an abundance of internal resources, looking and feeling good. Everything is going well and you are solving problems with ease.

Step 4 Self-belief

Complete this short routine with some affirmations to strengthen your self-belief. This will give you a powerful boost. Never rely on other people to give you this all-important feeling of growing capability – it's much more powerful when you do it for yourself. Without self-belief everything else you do will have uncertain results. Begin your affirmations with:

- I can ….
- I will …
- I have achieved …
- I am growing in my capacity to …

Recall past successes and remind yourself of the inner resources you used to get those results.

The more often you perform this exercise, the bigger will be the leverage you get from your innate resources until it becomes an integrated part of your mindset and your character.

Here are some more qualities to choose from. Select those that you feel will be most useful for you to have at this stage in your life and integrate them into your daily routine of mindset development.

- Focus
- Determination
- Flexibility
- Sensitivity

- Receptiveness
- Willpower
- Enthusiasm
- Drive

- Creativity
- Calmness
- Rationality
- Spontaneity

This is certainly not an all-inclusive list, so explore the qualities that you want more of to create your goal-beating mindset and work on them each and every day. Here are a few ideas.

- Construct your own affirmations, e.g. 'I will be more focused on my goals'; 'I am becoming more sensitive to other people's needs.'

- Recall times where you have had a particular resource, bring those experiences into your mind, and feeling good about having them today.

- Think of practical things you can do to develop a resource as part of your future goal plan. Look for opportunities each day that call for use of the resource you want to develop.

- Learn from other people who seem to have an abundance of the resource you want.

Energy

The levels of energy you have during the day will influence what you do and how you do it and this will directly impact the effort you put into achieving your goals. If your energy is low there is a danger this will affect the quality of your thinking and interaction with others, so it will be to your advantage if you can find a way of increasing your energy levels naturally. First of all take a look at your lifestyle. What is your diet like? Are you eating healthily and is your intake of alcohol at a reasonable level? What you put into your body has an immediate effect on your energy, so this is well worth reviewing, even if you think you have a healthy diet. If you are unsure about this it is very easy to consult a dietician or find the information you need from books or on the internet.

What you put into your body has an immediate effect on your energy, so this is well worth reviewing, even if you think you have a healthy diet.

Think also of the amount of exercise you get, particularly if you work in an office. Be careful not to go overboard on this – it's very easy to take too much of the wrong type of exercise and end up with even less energy. You could join a fitness centre, or alternatively take up something like yoga, tai chi or qigong, which will exercise both your body and your mind and help to develop clarity of thinking and concentration.

Do you take enough time away from work to re-energise your batteries? What are your natural work/rest cycles? Some people can be in work mode for many weeks without a break, while others require more frequent rest periods. Don't push too hard. Listen to your body – it will tell you when it's time to relax. You may notice other people working long hours and taking very short, infrequent breaks and want to do the same. It's best not to compare yourself with others, but to find the balance that's right for you. Energy cycles differ greatly among people, so if your energy is quite low, learn to get the most out of it without pushing too much, otherwise you may become over-stressed and this will eventually make you ill. Get a good balance of diet, exercise and rest, and be comfortable with the energy you have. You don't have to dash around doing myriad things to achieve your goals. There is a smarter option.

Sometimes low energy can be caused by a lack of purpose or enjoyment. A goal without a clear purpose is a goal without a meaningful human benefit in mind. There are many examples where people are working terrifically hard at achieving lots of small goals, but they are often tired, and underneath it all they are unhappy. Something is missing

from their life, but they rarely slow down for long enough to find out what it is.

> Lee has been achieving goals for the past five years. First it was new skills, then different jobs, then a new house, holidays abroad, house extensions, decorating and redecorating, and learning new IT skills along the way. There was no room for anything else in his life, and he always looked like there was something missing. One day he said that he had no sense of purpose any more. You will find him today running his own bar in Spain with his wife and enjoying a relaxing and happy life – which is his purpose for getting out of bed each day.

Whatever your goals are, make sure they are connected with a strong sense of purpose and you will find the energy you need to succeed. Your purpose will also help you choose goals that will be good for you and that you will enjoy achieving. It will help you to muster the energy to go that extra bit further and see something through to completion at times when energy is at a low level. The following questions will help you to find your sense of purpose if you do not yet have one.

- Why do you do what you do?
- What higher purpose do your goals serve?
- What words describe the highest expression of you as a person in all life contexts?
- What would you like to be remembered for?

The energy you give out will be interpreted by people around you as an attitude, and the more you work at creating and maintaining a positive, empowering mindset, the more you will emit a positive attitude that is inviting and attractive to others. The only people who like negative attitudes are people with negative attitudes.

Removing the barriers

Imagine you have enough knowledge and skill, and a real winning mindset, with plenty of energy, and you are progressing towards your goal. Then one day a small thought floats into your mind suggesting you could be headed for a fall. Over the next few weeks the thought gets bigger and attracts other similar thoughts until there is a cluster of thoughts, each one creating negative emotions attached to your goal. Now you have doubt, fear and limiting beliefs blocking your journey to success. No matter how well prepared, disciplined and organised you are, these barriers will prevent you from realising your true potential. That's why it is important to recognise these up front and find ways to overcome them.

Fear

"Many of our fears are tissue-paper thin and a single courageous step would carry us clear through them."

Brendan Francis

Fear is about the future. It is the mind conjuring up negative possibilities to prevent you from taking a certain action. It is more often fear of what you imagine rather than fear of reality itself that holds you back. Linguistically it takes the form 'what if it doesn't work out?' or something similar, and is more likely to manifest emotionally in the gut as a general feeling of unease or discomfort. Fear is an irrational emotion – it has to be, as it deals with a potential future, that is, something that isn't happening. Fear is a darkroom for developing negatives. Its intention is to protect you, yet it serves only to stress, limit and destroy. Fear has been described as a False Experience Appearing Real. It is all in the mind – and knowing how the mind creates its own reality, if you allow fear to take control you are likely to end up getting what you fear most of all.

A thirsty dog approaches the edge of a lake but is startled at the reflection it thinks is another dog and so runs away. The dog tries again and again to drink from the lake, but is prevented from drinking by its own reflection. Eventually the dog becomes so thirsty that it overcomes its fear of the dog in the lake and dips its nose into the water, only to find that the dog in the lake immediately disappears from sight and from mind.

The only thing that fear and your goal have in common is that they are both futures created by the mind. The type of thinking that will make your goal a reality is creative, rational and positive. The type of thinking your fear brings is destructive, irrational and negative. If you allow fear to take hold you will muddy your thinking and become indecisive.

When you have fear you have three choices of how to deal with it:

1   Live with it (not very pleasant).

2   Drop the goal associated with the fear (weak option).

3   Get rid of the fear (you will feel good as a result).

EXERCISE   Dealing with your fears

Cast off the chains of fear. Here are a number of ways of getting rid of fearful thought clusters.

1 Play with the fear

Whenever you become aware of a fearful thought, relax yourself and tell the thought that it may come to play with you but it will never occupy your heart.

2 Banish failure from your life

What could you achieve if you knew you couldn't possibly fail? Fear of failure is a frame of mind. You will never fail if you learn from experience, as everything

you do provides information and feedback to help you improve. So, there is no failure – only daily experience and feedback. Retrain your vocabulary to replace the word 'failure' with more positive words. Bite your lip whenever you catch yourself saying the word and restate in the positive.

3 Work with your mind-images

When fear takes hold, the mind-images that make up your thoughts can become dark and grey. Bringing positive colourful images of success into your mind with an inner smile will eradicate any dark images and boost your motivation to pursue your goal. Create a number of positive colourful success-images in your mind and meditate on them often. This will create a positive mind-energy, far stronger than any fear that may be trying to invade and contaminate your thoughts.

4 Imagination

If you find yourself thinking about all the things that could go wrong or all the possible risks, imagined or otherwise, ask yourself, 'what else could happen?' and imagine a whole range of positive outcomes instead. Remember times in the past when you succeeded in overcoming your fears and achieved great results.

Denise: I often use the example of when I jumped out of a plane from 13,000ft in a free-fall sky dive and landed safely. For me it doesn't get much scarier than that!

5 Challenge your fears

Often it helps to consider precisely how your fear is affecting you, and your goals, right now. Think about how your fear might be stopping you from enjoying new experiences, holding you back from success or limiting you in other ways. And ask yourself, 'what am I losing, missing or not doing?'

How is your fear affecting you?   What are you losing, missing or not doing?

You might also pluck up the courage to seek opportunities to face your fears and overcome them. For instance, a fear of public speaking can quickly fade with practice and a number of successes under your belt!

Belief

How big is your world? What is the extent of your involvement and participation on the planet? We all know so much about the world these days from media bombardment, but how much of it are we actually connected with on a day-by-day basis? Why is this an important consideration, you may be asking? In a few moments we are going to ask you an important question that will make this very relevant, but first, imagine that you are physically connected to all the people you communicate with on a frequent basis, thus forming a visible network. What does your network look like? How much diversity of experience and capability is there in your network?

Now here's the question.

What do you believe are the limits of possibility for your future success?

You can answer this question within two contexts, the first being the world as defined by your existing network of contacts, and the second as defined by the unlimited extremes of your imagination.

> Some people live in very small worlds. They
> may be very well travelled and yet unworldly,
> having fixed ideas and being closed off to new
> experiences.

Some people live in very small worlds. They may be very well travelled and yet unworldly, having fixed ideas and being closed off to new experiences. As a result they live their life making very few changes, sustaining the same lifestyle year after year. There is nothing wrong or bad about this, in fact many people who live like this are extremely happy. But it is not likely to help you stretch and beat your goals.

When you look beyond your existing world and begin to extend your network, the only limit to your potential is your imagination and your belief in yourself. And you have control over both of these.

EXERCISE Making your future possible

1 Recall a time in your past when you faced a challenge that seemed impossible, and yet you succeeded.

2 Remember your thoughts and feelings before you succeeded, as you were perceiving impossibility.

3 Now remember how it felt when you'd successfully completed the challenge.

4 Tell yourself that impossibility comes before success, never after, and it's how you respond to those feelings that matters most.

❝Live by what you believe so fully that your life blossoms, or else purge the fear-and-guilt producing beliefs from your life.❞   John-Roger

Here are some empowering beliefs to get you into a 'beat your goals' winning frame of mind.

Believe ...

- in your unlimited potential;
- that other people want to help you;
- the future you see will become reality;
- you have access to all the inner resources you will need;
- in the power of your mind to create the future you want;
- your future experience will make you smarter and stronger;
- the world is full of helpful resources outside your current network and they are all available to you;
- you deserve to succeed.

If you have any beliefs that might be holding you back, use the following exercise to change them for something more empowering. The exercise has three steps. First, you will identify a limiting belief, then you will remove it, and finally you will replace it with an empowering belief. You may prefer to do this exercise with a friend. As you talk about a situation you find difficult or puzzling, your partner can listen for the statements of belief in the words you are using.

EXERCISE   **Harnessing the power of belief**

Step 1:

In the box below describe a situation where you are having difficulty making progress. It could be conflict with another person or an inner conflict where you are having trouble making a decision. It could be a personal block about something or it could be a difficult or puzzling person. Enter a heading for your situation at the top of the box and answer this question: 'What do I believe about this situation/person?' It is possible that you will come up with more than one limiting belief for any blocked situation. Avoid questioning or evaluating your beliefs at this stage. Absolute sincerity and honesty will produce the best learning and progress from this exercise.

Situation

Step 2: Challenging a limiting belief

One way to change a belief is to question its validity. If you question anything enough and gather contrary evidence, you begin to doubt it. Ask the following questions to challenge your beliefs in the box above:

1 Has there ever been a time when this belief was not true or did not apply? Think of some examples.

2 In what way is this belief ridiculous or absurd?

3 What will it cost me to keep this belief?

4 How would I be different without this belief?

5 What exceptions are there to the belief?

6 What caused me to have the belief in the first place? Do these assumptions still apply?

Step 3: Developing an empowering belief

Create a new and empowering belief statement, for example, 'I am capable of …', then find as many reasons, with as much evidence as possible, to support it. Strengthen this new belief by asking the following questions:

1 What evidence supports this belief?

2 When have I known it to be true?

3 Who do I know who has this belief?

4 What will happen when I hold this belief?

"A belief is not merely an idea the mind possesses; it is an idea that possesses the mind."

Robert Oxton Bolt

Additional resources are available from the Quadrant 1 website. Go to **www.quadrant1.com** and click on know-how.

▶ Breakthrough hidden limitations

▶ Reframing negative into positive.

The routine of your life

"The fixity of habit is generally in direct proportion to its absurdity.**"**

Marcel Proust

Much of what we do in life is driven by our unconscious habits, like when you have driven a car from A to B in autopilot mode and are unable to recall passing landmarks along the way. Or if, like most people, you procrastinate now and then, you may have lots of small things that you do routinely, in place of what you could be doing. When habit and routine are working well for us that's great, but sometimes we develop habits that limit and prevent us from having, doing or being what we want in life.

The effect of habit and routine can be explained with further reference to the motor car. You do not have to know how a domestic car works in order to get around in it, but if you were a racing driver behind the wheel of a high-performance sports car you would need to understand how the engine works and how to keep it tuned to deliver peak performance. If you are serious about becoming a serial high achiever, then like the highly tuned sports car, you will need an awareness of the parts of your life that you can tune for peak performance.

In this chapter we offer you the chance to explore some of your habits, identify any that are holding you back and create new ones to help you achieve your goals and desires. Think of this chapter as a short course on tuning your thinking and behaviour for improved performance.

Habitual thinking

"Whether you think you can, or whether you think you can't, you're right.**"**

Henry Ford

The way we think directly influences our success. Think about it. When your thoughts are focused on your goals, on what you're going to achieve and the benefits or rewards that will result, how do you feel? Now compare this with when you think about all the reasons why you might not succeed, the potential obstacles and the possible pitfalls. Which feeling do you prefer? Which thoughts will most help you beat your goals?

How you think affects your feelings and behaviour and your behaviour affects your results.

Thoughts → Feelings → Behaviour → Results

Example

Take tennis players. When we visited the Wimbledon tennis championships earlier this year we were privileged to see some of the most talented and skilled players in action. These world-class players are fully capable of hitting outstanding shots, and if they can hit one shot then they can hit many. So how is it that, when the pressure's on, or they get complacent, they can fail to perform at the same high level? Usually it's because they are beset momentarily by self-doubt or complacency. We've all seen it, the moment when the Number 1 seed misses a straightforward shot against an unseeded player. You only have to listen to the commentary of the experts discussing the mindsets and thinking patterns of the players to know that it isn't just talent and technique that separate the champions from the rest.

> **Be careful what you think about because, at an unconscious level, our minds do not differentiate between positive and negative thoughts.**

Furthermore, our thoughts are magnetic. What we think about we attract. Have you ever noticed how many more happy people you meet when you yourself are happy and smiling, or how many silver sports cars you notice when you're thinking about buying one? Be careful what you think about because, at an unconscious level, our minds do not differentiate between positive and negative thoughts. So, if you think about missing a shot in tennis you probably will, and even if you think about 'not' missing a shot, you probably still will because the mind deletes the word 'not'.

EXERCISE The effect of negative words and thoughts

Just for a moment, don't think about a pink elephant with purple spots. You see, you have to think about it first, in order to 'not' think about it.

Example

Denise was waiting at the cash dispenser of her local bank. The person ahead of her was getting more and more exasperated as he couldn't remember his PIN number. As Denise waited in the queue she thought, smugly, how she'd had the same PIN number for over 15 years and hadn't forgotten it once. And you've guessed the rest. When it came to her turn she got what she'd been focusing on and forgot her own number!

So, when thinking about your goals make sure your thoughts are positive and think about what you do want rather than what you don't want!

Habitual language

Like our thoughts, the language we use is habitual and we don't always think about the impact our words have on others, on ourselves and on our performance. Our language not only reflects our inner beliefs and thoughts, it has a direct impact on our thinking, our behaviour and our results. For instance, if we were to describe writing this book as 'difficult' then the chances are that's how we would be thinking about it. And even worse than that, the more we used the word, the more we would begin to believe that writing is difficult. Consequently, this might start to affect our behaviour so that we would begin to focus solely on the 'difficulties', ignoring what we can do easily and, ultimately, would fail to complete the book.

Our language contains many assumptions, some of which are intentional and others which are not. Very often these assumptions are unhelpful and reflect our deepest limiting thoughts and beliefs.

A Sales Director of a large organisation was preparing a speech for the sales conference where he was to announce the new corporate vision, culture and goals to the sales force. He asked Denise to give him some feedback and help with his presentation. He began reading to her and as he reached the end he finished with, '....and if this works just imagine how good it could be....' . She must have looked a little disappointed, as he wanted to know what was wrong. 'Well aren't you going to achieve this?' she asked. 'Of course we are,' he replied. 'Well why not say so? How about *when* we achieve ... imagine what it *will* be like.'

The mental images we create for ourselves and for others are so easily influenced, or contaminated, by the simple words we use, and all too frequently we don't even stop to notice. If our language does have such a powerful influence on our behaviour and results, how is it that we use unhelpful language so much of the time? Instead of giving yourself a

handicap when setting out to achieve your goals how about starting in pole position by fuelling your goals with positive, empowering thoughts and language instead?

Below are a few examples of simple changes you can make to your language and thinking that will help build the confidence and commitment to beat your goals.

Unhelpful language	Helpful language
If I finish this book	**When** I finish this book
I'll **try** to learn to speak French	I **will** learn to speak French
I want to **but**	I want to **and**
I **can't** change	I **can** learn how to change

EXERCISE The impact of language

Notice how many 'unhelpful' words you use in conversations and in your thinking, and recognise the beliefs or assumptions that underpin these words. Where these are unhelpful, select an alternative to use in the future and write in the space below.

Unhelpful language
E.g. 'difficult'

Helpful language
'not easy'

Reframing

As we've seen, negative thoughts will influence your energy and behaviour and can be picked up by others. You're going to achieve certain goals and in doing so you'll be making things happen. Along the way it's very likely that you will want to influence other people. For a moment, think of people whose influence you enjoy, and notice what their energy is like. How do others perceive your energy? Do you think they enjoy interacting with you? If you have any negative thoughts, or if you use negative language, how do you think this will affect them? When you are faced with negative thoughts, find something good and positive to focus on with whoever or whatever you're dealing with.

So, even though much of your thinking may be driven by habit, you do have some choice in what you think. Use the simple and effective technique of reframing to help turn negative thinking into positive thinking, focus on solutions instead of problems, have positive influence with others and move closer to achieving your goals.

❝I am neither an optimist nor pessimist, but a possibilist.❞ Max Lerner

A reframe is simply taking a different perspective, for instance seeing the glass as half full rather than half empty. Here are some questions to help you think of suitable reframes for negative thinking.

- Where *would* this be useful?
- What *is* good?
- What *positive* meaning could this have?
- What *can* I do?

Below are some more common examples of unhelpful thinking with suggested reframes for switching the thoughts from negative to positive. If you have come across reframing elsewhere you might ask yourself just how well you are doing and consider how many of your inner thoughts are actually positive and useful. Move on from the examples shown and reflect on your recent experience. Sometimes the simplest of techniques can be well understood intellectually but tough to actualise.

It's always raining	Isn't it good to know the plants have enough water?
I find this really difficult	Won't it be great when I've done it?
My life is so complex	Isn't it good to know you can manage all that?
No one understands me	What can I do to help them understand me better?
I can't do that	What *can* I do?
But ... it will never work	What would help it to work? What if it does?
This isn't what we want	What *do* you want?

EXERCISE Reframing your language

Think about a goal that you would like to achieve or are already working towards. As you think about it, notice any unhelpful thoughts that might stand in your way and write them in the space below. Now, create a question to reframe the thought into something more positive.

Unhelpful thought	Reframe question

Give yourself the best possible chance of success by making a habit of reframing and replacing unhelpful thinking and language with thoughts and words that give you a real boost. Remember, success is a personal choice, and it starts in your thoughts.

Habitual behaviour

Our behavioural habits are also driven at an unconscious level. Sometimes these are helpful and at other times they're not. Here we describe some of the patterns, called meta programmes, that can have a significant impact upon your ability to achieve your goals. As you begin to understand how the patterns work, you will benefit most by developing your flexibility and increasing your range of behaviour in order to get what you want rather than labelling other people as 'this' or 'that' type.

Meta programmes are unconscious filters that determine what we pay attention to and which influence our habits of thinking and behaving. There are no right or wrong patterns, although some are more useful than others in certain contexts. When you start to recognise your own preferences you will discover why your thinking and behaviour follow certain patterns and how this is helping or limiting your ability to set and achieve your goals.

 Remember, success is a personal choice, and it starts in your thoughts.

For each of the patterns we have included examples of how to recognise them in behaviour and language, and highlighted how they might be impacting your goal setting. Later in the chapter we offer some exercises to help you expand your range of behaviour by utilising some of the patterns you use least. When reading the following descriptions be aware that they refer to extreme ends of a continuum and it is likely that you will actually operate somewhere along the continuum rather than at the extremes.

Big picture or detail?

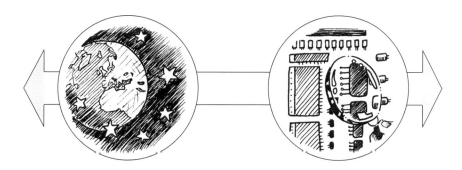

This pattern determines the chunk size of information you prefer to communicate with. Do you have a tendency to focus on the big picture and overall concepts or does the specific detail seem more interesting and appropriate?

Big picture

If this is your preference you will prefer thinking in concepts and overviews and have a clear idea of your overall vision and direction. While you may be willing to concentrate on detail for short periods of time, you may start to feel irritated with too much. You probably prefer to read a summary rather than a full detailed report.

Implications for goal setting

+ You will have a good overall understanding of how your goal fits in with the bigger picture of your dream.

– You may overlook the details necessary to help you achieve your goal.

Suggestions/tips

Before embarking upon your goal be sure to check the details to ensure that this is really what you want and that you have the resources to achieve it.

Example – imagine what would happen if you booked to go on a trip overseas and didn't consider the details regarding visa or vaccination requirements.

Detail

If this is your preference you will enjoy working with details and are unlikely to focus on overviews. You may perceive people who have a big picture pattern as being vague or having their 'head in the clouds'. You may sometimes find that you can't 'see the wood for the trees'.

Implications for goal setting

+ You will consider the specifics necessary to achieve your goal.

– You may lose sight of the overall goal, be distracted by unnecessary detail or find that your goal no longer supports higher goals or your dream.

Suggestions/tips

When you find that your progress is being slowed down or you're caught up in too much detail, ask yourself 'What's the overall purpose

or objective?' or 'What's most important here?' and refocus on what you want to achieve.

Make a note in the following table of some behaviours or habits you will keep, stop, do more of, and do less of, to balance big picture with detail for optimum results.

Keep doing ✔	
Stop doing ✘	
Do more of ✛	
Do less of ▬	

Away from or towards?

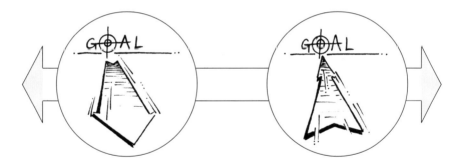

This pattern describes how people are motivated and, in particular, whether they want to *achieve* something or *avoid* something. When setting goals, the more specific you can be about what you want, the better.

Towards

If you are motivated 'towards' you will focus on targets and future goals. You may feel as if you are being pulled towards what you want and will talk about wanting, gaining, achieving and so on. Your goals and what you stand to gain from them may excite you. The downside is that you may overlook potential obstacles or problems and may fail to make contingency plans.

Implications for goal setting

+ You know what you want and have a clear focus on your goal.

− You may overlook potential problems and get caught out by unexpected obstacles.

Suggestions/tips

Take time to consider the possible pitfalls so that you can plan ahead or consult someone else who can do this for you.

Away from

If you are motivated 'away from' you may focus on what you 'don't want' or what you want to avoid. You may find that your motivation is triggered by problems, threats, deadlines or unpleasant experiences to be avoided. You will probably be very good at troubleshooting, problem solving and recognising obstacles. On the other hand, you may find that you lose sight of the end goal or experience a lack of clarity or focus around your goals, and instead focus more attention on what's wrong and what needs fixing.

Implications for goal setting

+ You will avoid repeating unsatisfactory experiences and foresee potential problems and obstacles that might prevent you achieving your goal.

– You may not have thought beyond what you don't want and be unclear about what you do want to achieve.

Suggestions/tips

When you find yourself talking and thinking about what you don't want or what you want to avoid, flip the coin over and focus on what you do want instead. Focus on the future, imagine what it will be like when you achieve your goal, and make it really compelling.

Make a note in the following table of the behaviours and habits you will keep, stop, do more of, and do less of, to balance 'away from' with 'towards' for optimum results.

Keep doing ✔	
Stop doing ✘	
Do more of ✛	
Do less of ▬	

Options or procedures?

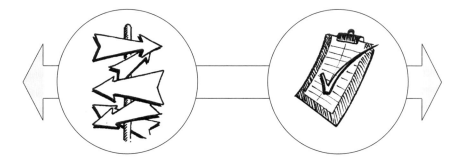

This pattern determines whether you like to consider all the possibilities or prefer to have a clear procedure for achieving something.

Options

If you have an 'options' pattern you will be motivated by opportunities, possibilities and choices and will seek alternative ways of achieving your goal. You may even have a range of goals. You will talk in terms of what 'can' or 'could' be done and will explore 'how else' you can achieve something. You are excited by unlimited possibilities and may enjoy new ideas and starting new projects. You may, however, feel less motivated to complete a project and will prefer to bend the rules rather than follow procedures. Beware: having too many options can lead to confusion, lack of focus and, ultimately, inertia.

Implications for goal setting

+ You will be good at brainstorming ideas, exploring possibilities and seeking better ways to do something.

− You may be reluctant to commit or close down options and may lose impetus to see an idea through to completion or follow the necessary process to get there.

Suggestions/tips

Allow time for creative brainstorming early on when selecting and setting goals. Then prioritise your options; focus on the most important one and find the best way to achieve it. You might even create a procedure to help you do this.

Procedures

If you have a 'procedures' pattern you will prefer following a set process and doing things the 'right' way. You may use language like 'must', 'should' and 'have to'. In order to achieve your goals you will want a clear procedure and steps to follow and will continue until the end. You may feel very uncomfortable about bending the rules.

Implications for goal setting

+   If you have a procedure for achieving your goals you will follow it consistently and ensure you complete each step in turn.

–   If there is no procedure or the process isn't working, you may lack the flexibility to create a better way of getting there. You may be pursuing a goal because you feel you 'should' rather than really wanting to.

Suggestions/tips

Create a process for checking that you are on track. Practise flexibility as sticking too rigidly to plans may cause you to miss your goals. When you find you are using words like 'mustn't', 'must' and 'should', ask yourself questions like 'What if I did?' or 'What if I didn't?'.

> In our experience this pattern creates an extremely powerful dynamic in teams, and has been responsible for numerous conflicts between people working towards the same goal. In any team effort you have a mix of preferences for procedures and options patterns. When you begin to understand how these patterns work you will be able to agree procedures for getting work done. This in itself is not sufficient to resolve conflicts, as there is a tendency for individuals to revert to their preferences unintentionally. So, the key to keeping on track is to maintain an ongoing dialogue so that any deviations from a plan can be openly discussed and next steps agreed.

Make a note in the following table of the behaviours and habits you will keep, stop, do more of, and do less of, to balance 'options' with 'procedures' for optimum results.

Keep doing ✔
Stop doing ✘
Do more of ✚
Do less of ▬

Sameness or difference?

This pattern influences how people react to change and whether they are motivated by new and different or familiar and consistent. When you look at the hat pictures above, do you see them as identical or different? Look closely.

Sameness

If you prefer familiarity, want things to stay the same and even resist change, you have a 'sameness' pattern. You may have a lot of similarity in your life and may visit the same restaurants, order the same meal, go to the same place on holiday and buy similar types of car, for instance.

Implications for goal setting

+   You may build on what you have done before and use proven methods for achieving what you want.

- You may not set many goals because you want things to stay the same as they are. If you don't set your own goals you may find you are affected by change generated by other people. Or your goals may be limited by your desire for familiarity.

Suggestions/tips

Look for ways of keeping the best bits, improving on what you have now, and recognise the common aspects between future outcomes and the present situation.

Difference

If you desire, even thrive on change, you have a 'difference' pattern. You like to seek out things and experiences that are new, unique and different. You will feel uncomfortable or bored when situations remain the same. You love to experiment and visit different places, have different experiences and do things differently from how they've been done before.

Implications for goal setting

+ You will seek new and different goals and ways to achieve them, and won't be limited by current circumstances or ways of working.
- You may seek change for the sake of it and dismiss what's already working well. You may lack the motivation to achieve a goal that is similar or repetitive.

Suggestions/tips

Build on what already works well, avoid wasting time reinventing the wheel, and identify differences between your goal and what you've done before.

Make a note in the following table of the behaviours and habits you will keep, stop, do more of, and do less of, to balance 'sameness' with 'difference' for optimum results.

Keep doing ✔	
Stop doing ✘	
Do more of ✚	
Do less of ▬	

Proactive or reactive?

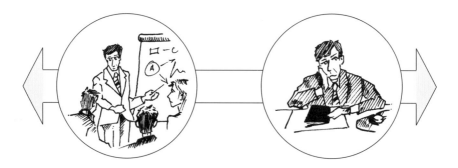

This pattern determines whether you prefer to take the initiative or wait for others to act first.

Proactive

If you have a 'proactive' pattern you will enjoy taking the initiative and may jump into situations without thinking or analysing. You will get the job done rather than waiting for others to initiate. You enjoy being active, making a difference and getting on with it. You may become restless with prolonged discussions that don't appear to be moving towards action. You will use language like 'When do we start?', 'Let's get on with it' or 'Let's move on'. On the other hand, you may not allow sufficient time for reflection and planning and may not think through the consequences of your actions.

Implications for goal setting

+   You are great at getting on with things, taking action and making things happen.

–   You may not think things through or consider the implications and may take action before checking that it is appropriate.

Suggestions/tips
Take time to consider the consequences of your actions or find someone who can ask questions to help you do this.

Reactive

If you have a 'reactive' pattern you will prefer to take time to consider ideas before committing to action and may wait for others to take the initiative. You may use words that avoid commitment like 'maybe', 'let me think about it' or 'perhaps'. At the extreme, people with this pattern may wait too long before acting and then find themselves reacting or 'fire fighting'.

Implications for goal setting

+   You will take time to think things through and consider the implications of your goals.

–   You may be slow to act or even miss opportunities altogether.

Suggestions/tips
Focus on what's important to you and on what you want to achieve, and then imagine how much more likely you are to succeed by taking the initiative more often. Remember times when you did not get the outcome you wanted because you waited for someone else to take the initiative.

Make a note in the following table of the behaviours and habits you will keep, stop, do more of, and do less of, to balance 'proactive' with 'reactive' for optimum results.

| Keep doing ✔ |
| Stop doing ✘ |
| Do more of ✚ |
| Do less of ━ |

Past, present or future?

This pattern explains where we focus attention – whether we dwell in the past, in the moment, or prefer to form conjectures about the future. This is different from the 'towards – away' pattern which has more to do with temporal aspects of motivation. This meta programme is more about the time orientation of our thoughts.

EXERCISE   **Past, present or future focus?**

With your eyes closed, draw three circles representing the past, present and future. Notice which is the largest. This is likely to be your main focus of attention in terms of time.

Past focus

If you place a lot of attention on the past then your emotions, experiences, conversations and decisions are likely to be influenced by past experience. At the extreme, others may sometimes describe you as 'living in the past' or seeing life through a 'rear-view mirror'. It can, however, be useful as a way of measuring performance and learning from experience.

Implications for goal setting

+   You will use lessons from the past and measure how far you have progressed.

−   You may be unclear about your future goals and miss opportunities in the present.

Present focus

When your attention is focused mostly in the present you will pay full attention to what you are doing and how you are feeling right now. You may have raised awareness and notice opportunities as they occur; however, you may not anticipate change or know what you want to achieve in the future, and as a consequence you may not move forward.

Implications for goal setting

+   You will be very focused on the task in hand and feedback you receive.

– You may not be driven to set goals or plan for the future as you are more interested in the here and now.

Future focus

With future focus you are likely to know where you're going, what you want in the future and what you need to do to get there. You may, however, overlook feedback in the present or recent achievements and will be too busy focusing on the next steps to appreciate what you have now or to celebrate your successes.

Implications for goal setting

+ You will be very focused on future goals and what you want.

– You will miss feedback, overlook achievements and fail to celebrate your successes.

Suggestions/tips

Ensure you have a balanced focus of attention appropriate to the situation and what you want to achieve.

Make a note in the following table of the behaviours and habits you will keep, stop, do more of, and do less of, to balance 'past' with 'present' and 'future' for optimum results.

Keep doing ✔
Stop doing ✘
Do more of ✚
Do less of ━

Through time or in time?

Continuing the theme of time, there are three further dimensions to be aware of:

1   The duration of passing time.

2   Conjecture of the future.

3   Storage and retrieval of past experience.

These three dimensions can be explained by looking at certain thinking and behaviour patterns known as 'through time' and 'in time'.

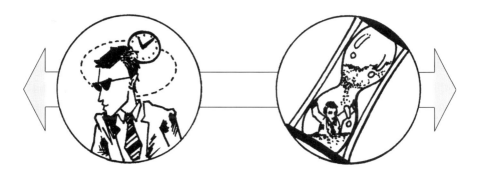

Through time

If you code time in this way you will be very good at planning and timing events to ensure everything gets done. Your diary will be well organised and you will rarely be late for anything. You may, however, become distracted from what you are doing in the moment by frequent tendencies to think about past and future events. You are likely to have an ability to recall most events in your life.

Implications for goal setting

+   You will be good at planning and time management, and be aware of all the steps along the way to your goal.

−   You may not give full attention to current activities when you're busy planning your next steps.

Suggestions/tips

Allocate time to focus purely on one particular activity and trust that future events are already planned.

In time

With this pattern your focus is very 'in the moment', which means that you give your full attention to whoever you are with or whatever you are doing right now. You may find, however, that meetings tend to over-run and that you are often late for appointments.

Implications for goal setting

+ You will be very focused on the task in hand.

– You may miss deadlines, fail to plan ahead, turn up late to meetings or be unclear about the steps towards your goals.

Suggestions/tips

Reserve some time each morning and evening to reflect on the previous day and organise yourself for the day to come, trusting that in the moment you will be able to give your full attention to the task in hand. Buy a small travel clock and place it in view as you begin each separate activity. Set a soft alarm to sound when you want to finish.

Make a note in the following table of the behaviours and habits you will keep, stop, do more of, and do less of, to balance 'in time' with 'through time' for optimum results.

Keep doing ✔
Stop doing ✘
Do more of ✦
Do less of ▬

Recognise your own patterns

You have probably identified some of your own patterns as you have been reading the descriptions. Here's a simple exercise to help you increase your awareness of your personal preferences.

EXERCISE Identify your patterns

How do you respond to the following simple questions? To help identify which patterns you have a preference for, go with the first answer that comes into your mind. Remember, there are no right or wrong answers.

When setting goals do you...

1 Want to see the big picture first or focus on the specifics?

2 Focus on clear targets or know what you want to avoid?

3 Prefer to follow a set process or consider different alternatives?

4 Look for unique and different goals or build on what you already have?

5 Take the initiative and get on with it or give full consideration and respond to others' actions?

6 Focus more on the future, the present or the past?

7 Focus more on what you're doing in the moment or do you have a clear plan for future events and actions?

Now that you are able to recognise your own patterns, notice which ones are helping you achieve your goals. If there are times where you feel they could be limiting you, expand your range and utilise some of the other patterns instead.

Expanding your range

The following ideas will help you begin to expand your range and increase your flexibility, and as you do this remember that your patterns are neither right nor wrong, it's more a matter of the degree of utility in support of what you want to achieve. If it's working, leave it be.

EXERCISE 1   Conscious practice

Seek out opportunities to practise using the other patterns. For instance, if you usually do a lot of through time, practise focusing in the moment, on one thing at a time, and ignoring outside distractions. Or if you like similarities, have a go at choosing something different next time you're in a restaurant or out shopping. Choose one pattern you'd like to practise and identify enjoyable opportunities for you to experiment.

EXERCISE 2   mental rehearsal

1 Choose a pattern you'd like to experiment with and a context such as work, studying or exercise.

2 Visualise a line on the floor with the two extremes at either end.

3 Choose a position on the line that represents your current pattern, for example: are you closer to options or procedures?

4 Stand on the line at this point and, in your mind, get a sense of what you see, what you hear, how it feels and how you're behaving.

5 Now walk towards the point from which you would like to be operating in this context. Get an image in your mind and notice what you will be doing differently.

6 If it feels comfortable then you've completed the exercise. If not, step back closer to where you started from and repeat.

Note: You can reverse the change by reversing the process. Make a change only if you really want to.

Additional resources are available from the **Quadrant1.com** website. Go to **www.quadrant1.com**, click on know-how and select the title you want.

- Meta programme questionnaire
- Reframing negative into positive.

For more information about the topics covered in this chapter see *NLP Business Masterclass* by David Molden, FT Prentice Hall, 2001.

The dilemma of choice

> "Analysis of over 25,000 men and women who had experienced failure disclosed the fact that lack of decision was near the head of the list of the 31 major causes ...."
>
> Napoleon Hill, *Think and Grow Rich*, Fawcett Books, 1990.

Imagine you are an archer, and you want to shoot an arrow at a moving target. You place the arrow, draw the bowstring and take aim. Then you track the target and find the bull's-eye ... and then you hesitate, and the target moves away from your line of sight, so you track it, all the time keeping the bow drawn in readiness, until your arm gets tired and you lose strength and lower the bow to relax your tired arms. You could have released the arrow perhaps two or three times, but for some unknown reason you didn't. As an archer you will only improve your success rate through practice, and to do that you must release the arrows from your bow. The alternative is to suffer tired arms, no results, and eventually you may lose the determination to continue with archery. Aiming for a goal can be like this sometimes. You set your sights on a goal, then ... nothing, inertia, because you didn't take the final decision that would release your energy and make things happen.

If you wait for the perfect, ideal moment to go for your goal, you may be waiting for ever. The ability to make and take decisions is often the make or break of a goal. You need to decide what you want, how to get

 If you wait for the perfect, ideal moment to go for your goal, you may be waiting for ever.

it and whether you're prepared to do what it takes to get you there. Once you've decided to aim for something, it's important that you remain focused, trust that you've made the right decision and keep on track. Achieving goals is a skill, and like archery, the more practice you get, the more successful you will become. So when you encounter inertia, it's often better to do something to move towards your goal and have the courage to learn from mistakes than lose whatever determination you may have at that point in time. It's not the goal itself that gets in the way, it's your thought process for setting and pursuing goals that makes the real difference.

"Until one is committed there is hesitancy, the chance to draw back, always ineffectiveness."
                                                                    Goethe

So what is it that prevents us from making decisions easily? You may remember a time when you had a decision to make that wasn't easy. It may have involved your career, moving house, a relationship, a business initiative or even where to go on holiday. You may have struggled to choose between options, or you may have felt uncomfortable with the inevitable decision you were about to make. We often call the process of 'not deciding' procrastination or indecision. When you become aware of how you do this, you can learn to replace it with a more useful strategy to help you make decisions more easily and effectively.

Frank and Jean were planning to start a business together and they were being very flexible and accommodating with each other at the ideas stage. Frank wanted to offer financial advice and training, as this was what he knew well, and he also enjoyed working with computers. Jean's background was in human resources and she wanted to provide HR consultancy and management training. For some time they struggled to shape a business offering that would include all these services. Whenever someone suggested dropping one of the services, inertia followed.

Neither Frank nor Jean wanted to discount their options, so they kept going over the same ground until eventually they agreed on a final description of their business and named it 'F&J Associates – *smart resources to help your business grow'*. Unfortunately, they never realised their ambitious sales growth because prospects were unable to identify exactly what type of business F&J Associates was in.

This kind of confusion is common in new initiatives. It's just as important to decide what you are *not* going to do as it is to decide what you *are* going to do. Holding on to all the options can create inertia, procrastination and confusion.

Conflicting priorities

Sometimes we find ourselves caught in an apparent dilemma between the devil and the deep blue sea – unable to make a choice between two alternatives, both of which seem equally important. You may have found yourself in the past being torn between X and Y. On the one hand you want to do X, and on the other you want to do Y. At one level, it may be that neither choice is satisfactory and you haven't generated enough alternatives to choose from, or that both are equally attractive, in which case whichever choice you make will be good, so what are you waiting for?

At another level, your indecision may be the result of a conflict in your priorities or values. Values are what's important to you, they form the basis of the judgements you make and drive your behaviour. It's no sur-

Values are what's important to you, they form the basis of the judgements you make and drive your behaviour.

prise then that when you experience a conflict of values you may feel that you're in a stalemate position and take no action at all, or you feel uncomfortable with the position you're in and the decisions you're making. A values conflict occurs where two values seem incompatible, for example work and family, money and freedom, security and excitement or independence and collaboration.

EXERCISE	Recognising inner conflict

Look through the following list and notice any conflicts that you have experienced in the past or are experiencing right now.

- Family/Work

- Money/Freedom

- Security/Excitement

- Relationship/Independence

- Independence/ Collaboration

- Doing things for yourself/Doing things for others

- Own goals/Others' goals

- Any others you are aware of.

If, for instance, you have a goal to set up your own business, you might potentially experience a conflict around the amount of time you spend on the business and the amount of time you spend with your family. If you allow this conflict to grow, you may ultimately risk sabotaging one or the other.

Michael, an entrepreneur, had started a business that was struggling to break even. The business had survived for two years on borrowed money, and Michael's accountant said he should sell up if he wasn't making a profit within the next nine months. Michael asked David to help, and pretty soon he had observed a conflict of values. Michael had employed two people who were not performing well. One was a designer, the other a sales executive, and he found it very difficult to motivate them both. Communication had broken down between the three of them, and this was the cause of further problems. Michael could no longer afford to employ them, but he kept trying to encourage them to improve. Things just got worse.

Michael loved to sell and he was good at it, but because of the mounting number of problems, he was spending less and less time prospecting for new clients – something the business really needed at this time. There was an obvious solution facing him, in that he couldn't afford to pay his people for much longer and that if he let them go (a kindness considering the fragile nature of the business and the abundance of alternative employment in the area), he could concentrate on sales and outsource the design work as needed. Instead he just carried on doing the same things. David was soon to discover that Michael's love of sales was equalled by his deep belief in the capability of people to perform, and this is what kept him stuck in a situation even though others could clearly see possible solutions.

When your values are driving you in opposing directions you can find yourself in a state of internal conflict where you feel discomfort with the present situation and an unwillingness to make a choice. In actual fact, as you become more aware of your higher values and intentions, and what's most important to you, you may find there is a great deal of overlap and common ground. For instance, seemingly conflicting prior-

ities in the example above of developing people and selling were providing Michael with a sense of entrepreneurship, but the roles he had created in the business were a barrier to its success. He was increasingly uncomfortable with his decisions, he could see only one way forward, and he worried about people's feelings. He was also very nervous when giving feedback about performance and he considered dismissing staff as a failure. When he refocused on why he was in business and what he wanted to get out of it, he was able to think more creatively about realigning the roles so that he could spend more time doing what he really enjoyed – selling.

Conflict resolution

In order to resolve these dilemmas and overcome the stalemate situation, you can negotiate, just as you would in a conflict between two or more parties, stepping up to a higher level where you have agreement and combining resources to achieve your common aims.

The following exercise is designed to help you reconcile the differences and recreate balance to help you move forward and make a choice.

EXERCISE Resolving inner conflict

This exercise works on the principles that, at a deep level:

- all our behaviour and thinking has a higher positive intention with our best interests in mind;
- separating the conflicting priorities enables us to deal with one at a time and clarifies our thinking around the problem.

Step 1 Identify a goal you want to achieve.

Step 2 Identify the conflicting values or priorities.

Step 3 Create an image of each value, what you see, hear or feel, and describe it in simple words below.

Value 1   **Image**   **Description**

_____

_____

_____

_____

_____

_____

_____

Value 2   **Image**   **Description**

_____

_____

_____

_____

_____

_____

_____

Step 4 Think about the first value and consider the following questions:

● Why is it important?

● What will it give me or do for me?

Continue asking these questions and writing your answers until you reach the highest positive benefit.

Step 5 Now think about the second value and consider the same questions.

● Why is it important?

● What will it give me or do for me?

Continue asking these questions until you reach the highest benefit. Continue stepping up for each until the highest intentions for both values are in agreement.

Step 6 Negotiate – ask 'How can both of these help me to achieve my highest value or intention?' Notice how this conflict may be getting in the way of achievement. How might they cooperate?

Step 7 Agreement – notice that the values have a lot more in common than you realised, so give yourself permission to integrate them.

Step 8 Create a new image for the integrated values and describe below.

New integrated values	Image	Description
		_____ _____ _____ _____ _____ _____ _____

If you're not sure about the answers to any of these questions, trust your intuition and take whatever comes into your mind. By reconciling your internal conflict, and recognising that each value involved in the conflict is well intentioned, you will find it easier to create a new higher-level value to move you out of the conflict situation and towards your goal.

The confidence to choose

Even when your values are aligned, and despite your skills, experience or expertise, it's still possible to make a meal out of making a choice! Here are some more reasons why people

struggle to make decisions, and some tips for increasing your confidence to make the right choice.

Too few options

Sometimes you can fall into the trap of believing that a choice of two represents a real choice when in fact it often presents a dilemma. If you are offered the choice of an Indian meal or a Chinese meal when you actually don't like either, this isn't much of a choice at all. When setting goals, whether in business or in your personal life, if you consider only two possible outcomes or ways of achieving what you want, you could risk missing the best option of all.

Linda was in two minds about how to make progress in her life and she had come up with two alternatives. One was to work harder at what she was already doing, the other was to give it all up and move to Australia, a country she was in love with. When she thought of the first option she could see only more stress and bad health. When she thought of the second option she worried about never seeing her family again. Neither option was complete enough to allow her to make a decision. Linda realised that the inertia of her thinking was creating stress, and by letting go of the urgency she had attached to it and learning to relax and appreciate what she currently had, she was able to generate many more possibilities and be more relaxed about making a choice that satisfied all her values around health, environment and family.

On other occasions you may feel you have no choice at all. This is often a matter of perception as we are making choices all the time, even when we don't realise it, and choosing to do nothing is still a choice. When you find yourself having to choose between two alternatives, neither of which is sufficiently motivating, or worse still you feel you have no choice in a particular situation, seek out additional possibilities by asking:

- How else could I do this?

- What else do I want?

Expanding the number of options available to you helps you see the whole picture and increases the likelihood of finding an alternative that is most appropriate and satisfies your higher values.

Too many options

On other occasions we can be faced with so much choice that we become overwhelmed and are unable to make the simplest of decisions, such as choosing a meal from an extensive menu, selecting a colour to decorate the home or deciding upon a course of action to resolve a problem at work. Prioritising goals is not so easy when you are faced with so many options to consider or you take the advice above too far and continue to seek out new options, even where there is no conflict, and make the process more complex than it need be. Focusing on too many options can result in a lack of progress or too little time or attention being allocated to each.

When faced with too much choice it helps to prioritise the options based upon your goals and criteria that are important to you, and remember, not choosing one option today doesn't mean you can never have that in the future, you just need to choose what you want first or at this particular moment in time. As you think about a choice or choices you are about to make, notice how you think about the situation and how you would illustrate it. You might try something like a mind map showing all the possible alternatives in no particular order. Try the following exercise.

Focusing on too many options can result in a lack of progress or too little time or attention being allocated to each.

EXERCISE   Working with choice

1 Create a mind map of all the choices you have now (see diagram below).

2 Start to prioritise based upon your goals and criteria and create a list with the most important at the top.

3 Check the order by comparing one alternative against another. Ask yourself, 'If I could have one but not two would that be OK?' and continue through your list until you are satisfied with the order.

4 Write out your new list.

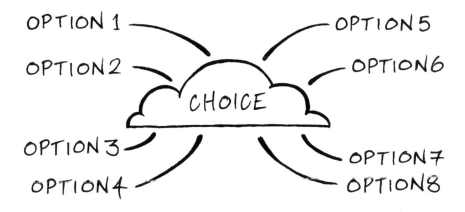

Priority

6 Go for promotion

3 Take on a new project

4 Enrol on a training programme

2 Engage a personal coach

7 Ask for a transfer

1 Get a new job

8 Start own business

5 Do some part-time consultancy

Use your imagination

In order to evaluate options effectively it helps to use all your senses to visualise each choice and imagine the outcome of these choices in the future. So before choosing what colour to paint your walls, imagine in your mind's eye what it will look like and how you will feel when it's finished, creating a vivid image of the result. Or when choosing what to eat in a restaurant, get a sense of what the meal will look like, how it will smell and taste and how you will feel when it arrives.

About a year ago David had the idea of providing a performance coaching service by e-mail. He piloted the idea among a group of existing clients and got excellent results. The next step was to design a system for making it available to larger numbers, and so he engaged some technologists to help him work this out. The solution sounded and looked very robust, until David began to imagine what the service would look like in the future, based on this design. What he saw was a room full of coaches bashing away at keyboards and a manager checking the quality of responses. He didn't like this picture at all. It just didn't feel right for him, and so working back from a more acceptable future scenario he redesigned the technology to give him what he really wanted – and what was most likely to work for him and for his clients.

EXERCISE   Let your intuitive imagination help you choose

Take one of your goals that you are working towards right now. Imagine you've chosen how to get there, and act as if you're already there. In your mind's eye get a sense of everything you see, hear and feel. Make this image as vivid as possible, and notice now that you have it whether or not it's what you really want and whether it has a positive feeling associated with it.

Unknown consequences

Even when you have a clear goal in mind, there may be steps and decisions you make along the way where the consequences are uncertain. For instance, you might decide to take on a partner in your business, or make a career move in a completely different direction. The only things in the future that you can predict with certainty are death and taxes, but if you are going to be successful you will need to be at least confident about your decisions. Use the following exercise to help you think about the consequences of deciding/not deciding to pursue a goal and to help you feel more confident about making that choice now.

Consider the consequences

Choose a goal that you are contemplating but haven't got serious about yet. Consider the following questions in sequence 1–4. Say the answers out loud and write them in the corresponding box.

❹ What will happen if I don't?	❶ What will happen if I do?
❸ What won't happen if I don't?	❷ What won't happen if I do?

Trust yourself

How many times have you gone ahead with something when deep down you knew it wasn't the right thing for you? At some level you know which is the best choice even when you're not consciously aware of it. Trusting your intuition and feelings is an important aid to making choices simpler.

| EXERCISE | Learn to trust your intuition |

1 Think of a time when you made a choice you weren't happy with. As you think about that time now, notice the feelings you are experiencing.

2 Now recall a time when you made a great choice and were fully convinced that you were right to do so, and again notice the feelings associated with that experience.

3 Describe each feeling and compare the differences.

Your intuition knows what is good for you and it communicates its wishes through feelings that give you a sense of congruity or incongruity. It will pay dividends to only make choices when you feel completely congruent about them. True congruence occurs when your choice or decision supports your beliefs, values and goals. It is a state of feeling sure, knowing what you want, being definite and trusting yourself. Incongruence is the state of having reservations and not being totally committed to a decision. You may feel confused, hesitant and unsure, or lack conviction. Learn to recognise your personal indicators for congruence and incongruence as these can be a valuable indicator of your commitment and confidence, and could save you mistakes and money! Where you notice feelings of incongruence before making a decision this might be a signal to check that the outcome is what you really want or whether additional information is needed. Ask yourself, what else do I need to be convinced?

Convince yourself

Another reason we don't find making decisions easy is because we are unaware of what we require in order to be convinced. When you remain unconvinced about a choice you may defer making the decision, feel uncomfortable about it or avoid it all together!

> Earlier this year David and Denise offered a new change technique to one of their clients, George, knowing that it would be just the right thing for his needs, but he was reluctant to explore it. Some weeks later he said that he had read some articles on the technique and it sounded interesting, but still no take-up. One day David used the technique with him and had an immediate result. From that moment on George was converted and asked where he could learn how to use it with his team.

We are all convinced in different ways. In George's case above it wasn't enough to hear or read about the new technique, he had to experience it for himself. Each person has a unique strategy for being convinced and it will consist of one or more 'convincers', i.e. ways in which you know at a deep level that it is ok to make a particular decision. Sometimes the strategy, or a part of it, can put a strain on decision making when the information available to you does not match the requirements of your strategy. What do you need in order to be convinced?

1 Information type

Most of us need to either **see** some evidence, **hear** what someone has to say, **read** reports, references, testimonials, or **do** something with the evidence. What type of information do you need to start to be convinced? Remember the last time you were convinced that someone was good at his or her job, for instance. Did you need to see the person in action, hear about their work from someone, read about what they had done, or actually get involved and experience it?

It's important to be aware of what you need to be convinced and then take steps to gather the appropriate type of information. For example, if you prefer written and verbal information you may be willing to select a conference venue from a brochure alone, whilst someone else might need to visit the venue and check its facilities in person before being able to choose. Similarly, when considering a promotion or role change, one person may make a decision upon speaking with someone about the new position, whilst another may ask to spend some time on the job to get first-hand experience before deciding.

2 How you use information

Once you know the type of information you require it is helpful to know what you like to do with it in order to be convinced. As you read the following descriptions, notice your preferences.

Automatic This means you are likely to be very decisive and make immediate choices and decisions, probably based on a small amount of information. So, provided you have seen, heard, read or experienced some evidence once, you will be convinced. You may find that you are willing to give people the benefit of the doubt, and in business this can be very empowering. On the other hand you could jump to conclusions, make hasty judgements or take unnecessary risks.

> **TIP** Check that you have obtained sufficient evidence and assess the level of risk involved before making an instant decision.

Number of examples You may need the information to be presented a number of times. This could mean that you will visit a shop two or three times, or visit two or three different shops, before being convinced to make a purchase, for instance. Or you may want to get two or three quotes, or be given feedback a number of times before being satisfied.

> **TIP** If this is your pattern, then seeking out your required number of examples in a shorter space of time will help you make choices more quickly. If you know you require three examples, then seek out three alternative proposals, solutions or ideas up front.

Period of time You may prefer to gather information over a period of time, dislike making instant decisions or 'need time to think about it'.

> **TIP** Ask yourself how much time you need to be convinced. What will you do with the time that will help you make a decision and how much more quickly can you do these things? Also, it can help to imagine the time has already passed. In your mind's eye, get a sense of everything you see, hear, feel and have done and notice if there is anything else you need, or are you convinced now?

Consistency It may be that you are never completely convinced and have a need to re-evaluate each time, having little or no consistency in the information you gather and the way you use it. You may even find that once you've made a choice or decision, you continue wondering whether there might have been a better decision you could have taken.

> **TIP** If this is your preferred pattern, simply acknowledging the fact will go some way towards helping. Also, ensure that you gather your preferred type of evidence and be aware that at some level the choice you make is the best one. Recall good choices you have made in the past, focus on what you want and avoid procrastination.

EXERCISE What does it take to convince you?

Use this exercise to check what convinces you. Think about a major decision you have made in the past, and consider the information you gathered that helped you make that decision.

How did you gather your information?

Observation	☐	Reading	☐
Experience	☐	Conversation	☐

How did you process this information to be convinced about the decision?

Automatically	☐	No of examples	☐
Period of time	☐	Never convinced	☐

When you know what your personal strategy is for being convinced, you will be able to move much more quickly and gather exactly what you need so that you can decide and move on. Each step in the information-gathering process should reveal more about your unique way of being convinced, and the more you learn about this, the easier it will be to beat your goals.

Additional resources are available from the **Quadrant1.com** website. Go to **www.quadrant1.com**, click on know-how and select the title you want.

- ▶ Conflicting priorities
- ▶ Convinced?
- ▶ The dilemma of choice.

External influences

The reasons people cite for not achieving their goals often relate to external factors such as 'not enough money', 'not having the opportunity', 'lack of support from others', 'other people's reactions' and so on. Sometimes excuses, sometimes perceptions, sometimes a reality. Yet even when these external barriers really do exist you can still influence your level of success by thinking and acting differently. This chapter looks at some of these barriers and offers ideas for overcoming them. It recognises that some people may have more to contend with than others, and success may seem a very distant dream, yet even the biggest of hurdles can be turned into driving forces for success.

Lack of opportunity

"A wise man will make more opportunities than he finds." Francis Bacon

If all roads seem blocked and there's no opportunity in sight, then some people might say, 'that's it' and take things no further. If you never had the chance, or it was never the right time to start your own company, sell your invention or idea, travel the world, learn a skill or meet the right partner, then it's just bad luck or lack of opportunity, isn't it? Or is it?

In the city of Oxford the public authority recently hatched a plan to turn certain city centre roads into pedestrian precincts and make others for the sole use of public transport. Local traders in that area protested against the plans, saying they would lose trade because customers could not park nearby. These traders clearly have a choice over their future. They can view the impending change as a threat to their livelihood, or as an opportunity to create new ways of finding customers for their products and services. Some of these traders have gone out of business, others have moved location, and some have taken advantage of the Internet as a marketing tool and are now serving a more widely dispersed customer base.

I wonder, in the above example, whether the traders that went bust were aware of the choices they had, or did they spend their time being concerned about the one choice that was being taken away? So, is opportunity and choice really an external factor, or is it more to do with the mindset you create in response to external events?

There is a story of a young Buddhist student who went to ask for guidance from his teacher. On entering the teacher's office he was greeted and immediately given a task. He was ordered to lift a large table made of brass with marble legs, which was standing by the door. After a number of attempts the student gasped, 'I'm sorry, but I can't lift it. It's too heavy.' Immediately the teacher corrected him, 'No. It's not too heavy, you're too weak. The table's weight is the table's problem. The fact that you can't lift it is yours.'[1]

1 Adapted from a true account in 'Nichiren Soshu Buddhism' by Richard Causton, Rider, 1988.

External factors clearly do have an impact on you and your goals, but if you focus too intensely on the problem it just gets bigger. In these situations, especially when the external obstacle is perceived as immovable, remember that you have two basic choices in how to respond:

1   Move the obstacle.

2   Move your thinking.

When the obstacle is obstinate, you can still remove it from your mind and release the power of your thinking. This is not so much about overcoming the obstacle, but rather of redirecting your energy onto creative ways to move forward and shape fresh, previously unimagined opportunities. When you consider the world's deepest problems, such as the Middle East conflict, Northern Ireland or Tibet, you find that the protagonists of the conflict are often trying to move the fundamental obstacles, yet while very capable are perhaps unwilling, or too ignorant, to move their thinking. With the knowledge and technological expertise at our disposal today it is possible to solve world hunger and misery. The only thing stopping us is our current way of thinking and talking about the problems. People of all races would have to reorder their priorities in order to unlock the capability to finding a workable solution. It is much easier to do this for yourself.

You may feel there is no opportunity to use your idea or to realise your ambitions – that it's never the right time, or that certain other things need to happen first, e.g. 'I'll begin when I have more time/the summer arrives/I'm feeling better/I move to the city …' etc. The more conditional you make the goal, the less likely it is that you will succeed – or you may not even take the first steps. Conditions are barriers, and the more you have, the more effort you will need to get things moving. While we certainly need opportunities for our goals to become reality, we can create them for ourselves.

Mark wanted help to achieve some personal goals, and during the first coaching meeting he told David that he frequently got headaches and was often tired. He attributed these things to a recent problem that had beset his business. The landlords had hiked up the rent by 150 per cent as the latest in a series of tactics to encourage the business to vacate the building. There were no suitable premises in the immediate area where he had built a loyal customer trade. He just couldn't find a way out, and the more he thought about it, the more tired and stressed he became. There seemed to be no opportunity to take the business forward.

Mark's personal goals brought a refreshing change of direction, and so he and David concentrated their attention on possibilities and choices, which helped to unstick Mark's thinking. Mark enjoyed the half-day in 'free thought' and he asked if he could try the same process on his business.

The following week there was another session during which Mark and his business partner brainstormed possible futures, while David made sure they kept well away from the problem that had been occupying both their thoughts for the past six weeks. The next day they decided on a new business direction and the problem ceased to exist. Mark told me how they had decided to stop wasting time worrying about the situation and complaining about the landlord. Instead, they took a fresh look at their customer profiles and created a plan to move the business into two new locations in an adjacent town, and market more creatively. The fresh energy that this decision created was amazing – an almost overnight change from stagnant to invigorating!

A shared goal

When the same goal is shared among a number of people, sometimes it may seem like everyone is pulling in the same direction, and yet there may be opposing undercurrents causing some individuals to veer off course. If your goals are linked with other people's goals and you are not having great success, the first piece of analysis we recommend is to check the alignment of key motivators that create the dynamics in relationships between the people involved. This is an activity in which many commercial organisations invest much time and money, as they know that misalignment between people and functions is often the cause of conflict and dysfunction. The levels of alignment involved here are: a) purpose, b) role and c) values and beliefs (see diagram below).

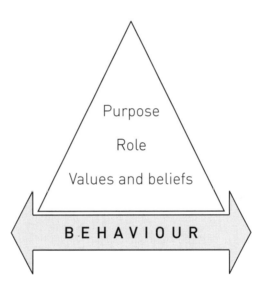

Each of these three levels has a bigger impact than the one below, such that companies that are able to connect employees with a common sense of purpose are rewarded with highly energised people who are both committed and loyal to the company. Yet the companies that achieve this are relatively few in number, growth being one of the biggest barriers to achieving and sustaining this high-energy state. The more people you have, the more effective communication you need. It is highly probable that people working towards a shared goal will have different purposes for their engagement.

 **The more people you have, the more effective communication you need.**

> Tom and Sue decided to set up a mail-order business supplying luxury gifts to companies that run incentive and reward schemes for large organisations. The high-level purpose behind Tom's decision is that the business will allow him to have the lifestyle he has always wanted. Sue's purpose is to be 100 per cent in the driving seat of her success. Tom's role is to travel the world in search of gifts to include in their catalogue and to generate sales. Sue's role is to set up the systems for sales and distribution. Together they will hire staff as required.

In this example Tom and Sue may have a strong relationship built on trust in each other and commitment to the company. Should this trust break down, it is possible that Tom's lifestyle and Sue's drive will begin to create a conflict of purpose – and this is conflict of the highest order, manifesting in the smallest of tasks and exposing other problems of role and values that may not have been apparent or seemed important when trust was high. In any competitive company, a stated common purpose can be very quickly relegated to a low-priority position as knee-jerk reactions to market changes kick in. Employees and customers are never fooled for long by meaningless mission and purpose statements that are not brought to life through daily actions.

It's rather like taking a group of children on a day trip, telling them the purpose is to have a good time, then yelling at them all day in an attempt to maintain control. If the purpose is to have a good time, yelling isn't going to help. So instead you might find a way of being in control that is aligned with the purpose of having a good time. For instance, why not make safety into a game? Make sure the children know what constitutes 'right' and 'wrong' behaviour, then award points to reinforce 'right'. Reward teams for their ability to stay close together, and deal with 'wrong' behaviour in a supportive, rather than a directive way.

Regardless of the emphasis put on stating a mission or purpose, it is behaviour that other people take note of and respond to, and behaviour is driven by inner values and beliefs. Differences between the things people say and do are not always recognisable as value and belief conflicts. Chapter 5 looks at the problems created when an individual's values are in conflict, and here we consider the effect of value conflicts in a team of two or more and the impact this can have on achieving the team goal.

The diagram below represents a group of four people who are working to achieve a common goal, in which they have each been involved in defining. Person A is being drawn off track by something that is more interesting than the team goal but not necessarily clear enough to be recognised consciously by A as a personal value. Person B is in conflict with person C and they have reached an impasse. Only person D is 100 per cent content with the journey to the goal.

Beliefs support values, and when we are involved in activities that feed our value system, we feel good and we are motivated to continue with the task. This strengthens the belief system and the entire process is self-reinforcing. Only person D is in this situation. B and C have dis-

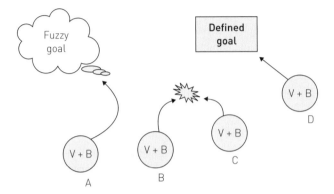

covered something more important to think about – each has a strong urge to protect their respective value and belief systems against invasion by the other. Person A is unaware of the inner conflict between the team goal and his unconscious fuzzy goal, but is likely to be enjoying the work of achieving the team goal less and less. Eventually A may also conflict with B, C and D.

Conflicts like these occur when individuals in a team work in isolation of each other. Attention is focused almost totally on personal tasks, without regard for the work others are doing. People may be working away quite happily and perhaps not totally in synch with the higher common goal. Discussions on purpose, values, beliefs and goals help to bind individuals into a cohesive team, and these aspects of goal pursuit will form part of the frequent dialogue among them. It is not enough to discuss and agree these things one time and expect the team to remain effective. Great team working comes from a clear and ongoing understanding of the goal, the higher purpose, changing priorities and working methods.

Win-win outcomes

When success requires the cooperation of others (and most times it will), the relationships you develop become interwoven in the fabric of your desires and your actions. Whatever goals you choose, at some level there is likely to be an impact on others or you will require cooperation and support from others in order to achieve them. Unless you put work into your relationships, they may act as barriers to progress. This means that you have to spend time building trust, while understanding and respecting others' needs and wants. If you just take from people, they will pull away from you. If you coerce them, they will avoid you. If you neglect them, they will forget you. If you trick them, they will talk badly of you. If you disrespect them, they will fail you. All these situations lead to a lose-lose situation. While it is possible to gain a win by these methods in the short term, in the long run you will lose. So, the best possible approach is to go for win-win outcomes from the outset.

Begin by building rapport and having the other person's interests in mind as well as your own. Put your own needs on the back burner until you have connected in some way, and then find a way of achieving a win-win. When other people gain from being associated with you, they will gladly continue to do so. So, when you are defining your goal, look for opportunities where all parties involved can benefit. If you are unable to find a win for someone, you may question why this person is involved and whether someone else may be better suited to assisting your cause.

Some people prefer to 'go it alone' and do it themselves, which may be perceived as being strong and independent. Actually, it's more a

> **If you just take from people, they will pull away**
> **from you. If you coerce them, they will avoid you.**
> **If you neglect them, they will forget you.**

strength to involve others because it requires a bigger effort by way of communication skills, inner resources and powers of influence. Believing that you know all there is to know, and that you can be totally self-supportive, is a major weakness in life.

Alison set up her own business, funded it herself, did all the work, hired temporary staff to do specific tasks, and delegated nothing further than this. After a good start she soon began to struggle, both operationally and financially, but she wouldn't ask for help. Eventually she succeeded, but only after taking advice from business consultants, in addition to having the stress of the many problems and broken relationships among staff. Success in this example was borderline, yet it could easily have turned into bankruptcy. The scope of Alison's success was clearly limited by her skill, knowledge and inward focus.

When you force things to happen, you create a situation that requires constant pushing. When you stop pushing, progress stops. Force also alienates people who feel they are being coerced or pressured in some way. You also may find yourself pushing against some very stubborn objects or attitudes, or trying to bring about a situation that just isn't ready to happen. When success comes easily it is usually because the ingredients of that success were ready to be brought together. It is far better to attract the resources, people and situations you want rather than push for them. This means you will be talking enthusiastically about your dream, desire and goal rather than merely explaining the detail of how you wish to engage people. It means you will be listening to people's ideas and involving them in your decisions rather than deciding alone. You will be engaging people in creative thought more often than in critical and evaluative dialogue. You will recognise when it is not the right time for a particular idea and when a person is unready or uninterested in engagement. You will know when to let go

and when to encourage activity. You will know when to use your powers of persuasion and when to let things happen more naturally. And above all, you will learn how to trust and how to support, enthuse and encourage others to be the best they can be.

About two years ago Angus set up a new business and gathered a team around him of people with complementary skills, who were each experts in their field – IT, marketing, finance, the law, etc. He made a special effort to include all the people who joined him in shaping the company, and very soon his goals became shared goals. He invested time in counselling the opinions of others, and developed business relationships and partnerships with people who had a clear benefit in helping his company achieve its goals. It was amazing how quickly this business got off the ground and evolved to become a very successful, multi-faceted enterprise run by people whose enthusiasm for setting and achieving personally challenging goals is highly infectious.

Anyone can devise a plan to create and launch an idea, initiative or a business. You just have to think about what you want and how you will go about it. This much can be done alone. Putting the plan into action requires very different abilities, not least the ability to connect with other people and persuade them that you are worth getting into a relationship with. After all, your personal qualities, skills and mindset are what will create success, not your plan. And if your plan doesn't work, you can always create another.

"You can have everything you want, if you will just help enough other people get what they want."   Zig Ziglar

Being a cause not an effect

There will always be external factors involved in the pursuit of any individual or shared goal. But regardless of whether they are coming from imposed conditions, blocked opportunities or other people, they can all be overcome. How you think about them and deal with them can make all the difference between achieving your goal and having your goal elude you. In any relationship, whether a business or social context, you can be in one of two positions: 1) cause or 2) effect. You are either being proactive in causing things to happen, or you are responding to the causes around you and feeling the effect of their influence on you and your goals. The difference between the two is to be found in mindset and behaviour. So, when thinking about achieving goals you clearly want to be 'at cause' rather than 'at the effect' of other people's decisions, and this may require a shift of thinking.

❝If you habitually react or respond to circumstances, where does the power lie in these situations? It clearly lies outside you, in the circumstances. Therefore, because the power does not reside in you, you are powerless and the circumstances are all-powerful.❞   Robert Fritz

This principle of cause/effect applies throughout this book and throughout your life. When you act and think from a position of being at cause, and you are making personal choices, you are being true to yourself, at your most powerful and open to more opportunities. In contrast to this, when you are at effect, you are reacting to others, using habitual responses, limiting your potential, perhaps blaming others, finding excuses for failure and allowing other people and situations to get in your way.

A common example of being at effect is when you are in a relationship that isn't good for you and you avoid ending it because you are more concerned about the other person than about your own well-being. You do things you don't really want to do because others want you to, and go from day to day fitting in with events as they arise.

Another common example is the person who continues in a job which gives them no enjoyment but has an element of security. There is a sacrifice here – personal power and choice are given up for the safety of a regular pay cheque. Even though the person may have made that choice, sometimes an exercised choice like this one removes the possibility for further choices being made. Choosing to stay put is not wrong – just be aware that it can disempower and stifle your energy.

Being the cause of events in your life puts you in charge of the choices you make and in the driving seat of your future.

Problems are gifts

A life without problems is unheard of. When we make progress in our life it is often the result of having confronted a difficult situation. The very problem that you are facing can be the one thing that helps you make the next significant move towards your goal. Without problems you do not have to try very much at all. A problem tends to stop you temporarily, and this is a great opportunity to try out some fresh thinking. You have seen how to reframe negative thinking in Chapter 4, and you can apply the same technique to open up problems and create a range of possible solutions. First, define what you think your problem is and then ask yourself some simple questions:

Without problems you do not have to try very much at all.

- How else can I view this?

- What else could this mean?

- How can this be a blessing in disguise?

- What positive effect can this have on me and my goal?

The following examples will give you an idea of some typical problem reframes. Notice how the responses unblock the problem and offer alternative perspectives on the situation, offering you the 'gift' that lies within.

Problem: We have no option but to keep our heads down until the recession is over.

Reframe: I wonder what potential there might be for business development in the way people usually respond to a recession?

Problem: I want to start my business but I can't get the money I need.

Reframe: Not getting all the money I wanted means that I can plan my start-up with much less debt.

Problem: There's little chance of getting promotion here because I don't have an MBA.

Reframe: Not having an MBA means that I will be promoted for what I have achieved in business, not for the credentials I have acquired. If this company doesn't see that, I'll find one that will.

Problem: The big players in the market are preventing me from growing sales above 5 per cent per annum.

Reframe: Because other players in the market are so big, I can find ways of responding to market changes much more quickly and flexibly.

Problem: I'm finding it difficult to make progress in my new business because very few people have heard of me.

Reframe: Being unknown gives me an advantage as there will be cus-
            tomers looking for something new and different, and I'm
            just the person to supply them.

Find the spark that ignites creativity and opens the path to the future

Even when problems seem insurmountable, there is always a way out
if you can find the one thing or the spark that gets you onto a positive
track towards a creative solution.

A local café owner was losing trade to a new competitor who had set up
a similar café in a location that was more convenient for passing clien-
tele. For some months the owner worried about falling sales and began
to look for ways of reducing his costs. One day he was explaining his
predicament to a customer when a new idea suddenly sparked a fresh
burst of enthusiasm. As his café opened only during the day, he decided
to share the lease with a new business partner who set up an Indian
restaurant and take-away service in the evenings operating from the
same premises. The new venture was called 'The Spice Café' and it not
only reduced the operating costs of both enterprises, it also brought
them new customers.

Ideas will come to you if you are open to receiving them. One sure way
of protecting yourself against new ideas is to fill your head with limiting thoughts and 'I can't' dialogue. If you remain open and optimistic,
ideas will come, often from the most unexpected places. If you ever find
yourself boxed into a corner, go and talk to people about your situation
and then listen to their responses with an open mind. If you evaluate
every idea as it comes to you, you may never get to the one idea that
could help you. Often the best ideas are developed from a spark that
may seem unworkable on initial evaluation.

"You never really get an opportunity. You take an opportunity."

James Cameron

Additional resources are available from the **Quadrant1.com** website. Go to **www.quadrant1.com**, click on know-how and select the title you want.

- Personal alignment
- Team audit
- 10 techniques for creative problem solving
- Getting buy-in to your ideas.

CHAPTER 7

Creating your success

> "Set your sights high, the higher the better. Expect the most wonderful things to happen, not in the future but right now. Realise that nothing is too good. Allow absolutely nothing to hamper you or hold you up in any way."
>
> Eileen Caddy, *Footprints on the Path*, Findhorn Press, 1991

What is it that you want? Is it something really compelling and worth pursuing? Is it something you're really committed to? Do you feel a sense of excitement as you think about all that you can achieve? Or are you not yet certain what your goals are?

In the early chapters we looked at the links between your dreams, desire and goals. Now you have the opportunity to discover exactly what you want and create the energy, drive and strategies for achieving it. Now that you know how to overcome limitations and tune your performance, you have arrived at the place where you will draw on your unlimited capability to create the shape and look of your future success.

It's time now for some fun and excitement as you get to focus on all the things you'd love to do and find ways of making them happen. You can choose to go for what you really want and enjoy your success or you can decide to settle for less and keep your dreams locked away. The only thing that could possibly be stopping you at this stage is the courage to take the first step, and if you're reading this, then we know you want to make the best choice and that you are ready to take that step now. So, having cleared and prepared the path, get ready to pave the way to limitless possibilities.

Decide on the results you want, take action and begin the journey to beat your goals!

In this chapter we offer you a simple formula and a range of strategies for turning your goals into reality. There is no rocket science to being successful; you just need a modicum of common sense, a winning mindset and the will and determination to keep going. With limitations overcome and performance tuned, the hard work has been done. From here on you will plan your journey using strategies that have worked for many other successful people. Some of these strategies utilise rational, conscious and logical ways of thinking. Others rely on a more intuitive approach. Knowing which to use will very much depend on your situation and what you feel comfortable with. And if what you're already doing is working, then carry on!

Aiming high

" If you can dream it, you can do it ... "   Walt Disney

People who consistently aim higher usually get higher. Unless you come across a rare streak of luck, you are unlikely to achieve anything more than what you aim for. Imagine that the choices before you are like a mountain range. Some peaks are quite low, while others are higher than the clouds, and routes to the top of each peak vary from gradual inclines to sheer rock faces. Once you have chosen which peak to climb and the route you will take, you have programmed yourself to achieve that aim, and all your efforts will be geared to that end. So,

> **Once you have chosen which peak to climb and the route you will take, you have programmed yourself to achieve that aim, and all your efforts will be geared to that end.**

before making that commitment it's worth getting into a creative space to make sure you set your sights on the most attractive, enjoyable and rewarding peak in the mountain range.

Have you ever experienced times when you haven't achieved the goals you set for yourself, or ever felt that you could have done even better? When we don't achieve what's  truly possible it can be because we're not thinking big enough, or we have great ideas and don't put them into practice, or we do all of this and still manage to overlook some of the detail and potential pitfalls.

A formula for success

It is not so difficult to achieve a one-time success. If you aim for enough targets you will probably hit one of them. This is the scattergun approach used by people with fingers crossed and eyes shut, hoping for a result. If you want to be habitually successful, you need to do more than cross your fingers and hope. You need a strategy or a formula – one that will give you the best possible chance of being successful in whatever you choose to do.

There are betting formulas, investment formulas and all kinds of business improvement formulas. What we are offering you in this book is not a tightly defined formula or a prescriptive list telling you what to

do, but rather a set of ideas and techniques from which you can create your own success formula. It contains a variety of techniques that are commonly used by successful people, which will help you to aim for the peak of the highest mountain, have all that you'll need to reach it, and be fully prepared to overcome any setbacks along the way.

The main framework uses thinking drawn from one of the most creative and successful business people of our times – Walt Disney. It is the same framework that Walt used to create and bring to life all the famous Disney characters you will find in his films and theme parks around the world, and consists of three key stages: Dreamer, Realist and Critic. Modelled by Robert B. Dilts, it is presented in his book *Strategies of Genius.*[1] We are sure you will also recognise it as a sensible high-level strategy for setting and beating your goals.

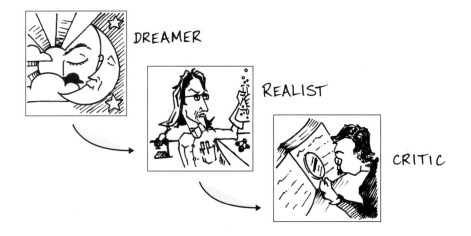

DREAMER

REALIST

CRITIC

To beat your goals consistently, it's important that your thinking and planning address these three key stages. Great ideas alone will only become a reality with appropriate checks, plans and actions. Unless you expose these to critical evaluation you may never find the devil that so

1 For further information about the creative genius of Walt Disney, read Strategies of Genius (Volume 1) by Robert B. Dilts, Meta Publications, ISBN 0-916990-32-X.

often lurks in the detail. If you skimp on any of these three key stages you are reducing your chances of succeeding. Favouring practicality over creativity could mean that you make an idea work and yet don't quite reach the highest peak. Time spent being creative without a practical action plan may mean you falter soon after taking the first steps. Too much attention to detail will make for a safe ascent, but you may never reach the peak. So, best results will be gained by focusing on one at a time, Dreamer > Realist > Critic. Underpinning all of this, remember to include in your mindset a focus on solutions and not on problems; be open to possibilities rather than barriers; work always from a positive intent; and not least, trust that your intuition will keep you on the right path and let you know if you begin to stray.

Stage 1 – the Dreamer: deciding what you want

"Would you tell me please which way I ought to go from here?" said Alice.

"That depends a good deal on where you want to get to," said the cat.

"I don't much care where..." said Alice.

"Then it doesn't matter which way you go," said the cat.

Alice in Wonderland, Lewis Carroll

If you can't decide which mountain to climb or which route to take and you set off directionless, where you will end up is anyone's guess. This is a great strategy for living a life of constant surprises – whereby a certain percentage will be unpleasant – and there would be only one person to hold responsible for the consequences: you! Common reasons why people don't achieve their goals include:

- They don't know what they want.
- They are pursuing the wrong goal.
- The goal isn't inspiring or compelling enough.
- They haven't thought it through carefully enough.

In the world of business, when the end goal is unclear, projects fail, discussions break down, results are disappointing, or people just lose sight of what they are supposed to be achieving.

A large finance company installed a new computer system. The purpose of the system was to help the company achieve a goal of increasing sales by collecting specific customer information. Post installation, the project for ongoing development became driven by the IT department, which focused on what users could and could not do on the system. People eventually lost sight of the overall goal, which was for non-technical sales people to gather customer information and sell. This is a classic example of how easy it is to stray from the original goal when you become distracted by the detail.

Have you ever noticed how some people seem to find opportunities where you would least expect? It's all to do with awareness and what they pay attention to. For a moment just remember when you last bought a new car and recall how many more of the same make and model you noticed on the roads around that time. And yet these models were always there. So how come you hadn't noticed them before? With all the information that surrounds us at any one time we can only ever pay attention to a limited amount, so whatever isn't relevant we filter out. As soon as the car does become relevant, your unconscious filters begin to gather the information instead of blanking it out and you develop a heightened awareness of something that was previously not a part of your life but is now.

With all the information that surrounds us at any one time we can only ever pay attention to a limited amount, so whatever isn't relevant we filter out.

The same principle applies with goal setting. Once you know what you want or the direction in which you're heading, you begin to recognise new opportunities connected with your goal that you wouldn't have noticed before.

An entrepreneur in the US decided to set up a business providing financial and legal advice to small companies. During the market research stage she realised how many small companies were run from home, with little or no secretarial support. This insight led to the creation of one of the first cyber-PA services for home-based business professionals.

The first stage in the process, therefore, is deciding what you want. Starting with the Dreamer allows you to really consider all possible ideas, open your thinking and set your sights higher – to find the peak that will give you the biggest buzz. If you miss this stage at the beginning you might limit yourself by basing your thinking on what you already know or what's familiar. If you really want to raise the stakes and beat your goals, get creative up front.

To get the best from the Dreamer stage you want be in a creative state of mind, one that is playful and free-thinking. In this state you will have an open mind about what's possible and be unhampered by practical limitations. You can let your imagination run free and look for new and different ideas or solutions.

You can create this state by:

- using your imagination – thinking in pictures;
- creating a story or metaphor;
- avoiding any evaluation or judgement;
- being playful and experimental;

- physically moving around;

- being relaxed;

- clearing your mind.

In the strategies section of this chapter we'll give you some effective methods for getting the most out of the Dreamer stage.

Stage 2 – the Realist: making it happen

The second stage of the process is the Realist. This is where practical steps are found that turn ideas into reality. This involves evaluating the creative ideas generated from the Dreamer, finding ways to make them work and putting plans in place.

> Simon, the wealthy chairman of an IT company, was reflecting on his personal success. He talked about how his friends would frequently mention the ease with which he had accumulated such wealth. This caused him some frustration because many times he had given them great money-making ideas, ripe for the moment, but never would they take up even one because they lacked the motivation to put a great idea into action.

While action is clearly necessary for any idea to have a chance, sometimes the desire to take action can come too quickly. To get the most from the Realist stage you want to adopt a state of mind in which you are thinking about the practicalities and all the possible outcomes of the actions before taking that first step.

You can create the Realist state by:

- questioning concepts and ideas;

- searching for any over-simplifications or omissions;

- asking how, what, where and when:

- 'How will this work in practice?'

- 'What exactly needs to happen?'

- 'What will the outcome of this action be?'

- 'When is the best time to begin?'

- 'Where will we have most impact?'

- 'Where will this result get us?'

- considering what other resources may help;

- suspending judgement and evaluation;

- focusing the mind on 'ways to make this work'.

Stage 3 – the Critic: have you thought of everything?

This stage of the formula is critical of the solution reached by the Dreamer and Realist in a way that seeks to strengthen. In this state you can see the vision, accept the details and see the pitfalls.

A company was recently set up to provide a project-managed office-moving service to city organisations. In the first couple of years there were many problems caused by the unforeseen details of client requirements at new premises. These were details they had not imagined when first designing the service offering. Luckily, they were smart enough to learn from this experience and later began to charge a fee for providing a detailed client survey prior to accepting a project. Had they been more critical of their service before starting up, they could have increased their sales by 10 per cent and reduced losses by a similar amount.

In the role of Critic you will err on the side of caution. The Critic is valuable in ensuring ideas and plans are made more complete, robust and foolproof. The Critic state of mind will focus on the details of the

solution, the fine mechanics and the practical applications. Orientation is towards what could go wrong and checking for contingency plans.

You can create the Critic state by:

- questioning the underlying assumptions;

- asking 'What would happen if…..?' and 'How do you know that …?';

- running through an 'as if' scenario and looking at the details;

- taking an observer's perspective;

- looking for what's missing;

- following the logic and testing for weaknesses;

- strengthening concentration on each detail in turn;

- seeking to strengthen rather than attack ideas and plans.

It's important to use this framework in the right sequence. Imagine starting with Critic: you'd be lucky to get off the ground. You'll recognise all the pitfalls and potential problems, but you will also limit your creativity and ability to reach for the stars. If you start with Realist you'll have lots of ideas around how to make it work and will be keen to get going and make things happen. You may, however, miss an opportunity to really expand your thinking and achieve even more than you thought possible.

Starting in Dreamer allows you to consider all possible ideas, open your thinking and set your sights higher. And when combined with some useful Realist and Critic thinking you'll put the necessary steps in place to make sure you turn your dreams into reality.

Strategies for the Dreamer

Nothing is more dangerous than an idea when it's the only one you have. You may be eager to get to the details, but it is well worth taking some time to open up your thinking and consider all the possibilities. You want to make sure that before you get stuck in you choose the goal that will boost your motivation the most. Don't settle for half measures here. It either feels good or it does-n't. The stronger the feeling, the more compelling it will become as you think about achieving it. Is it really what you want? Does it match your values and does it support your higher goals? These are all worth con-sidering and if the answer to any of these questions is 'no', then you may want to stretch your thinking.

Why do any of us do any of the things we do? Why do we set goals for ourselves? Usually it's because there is something greater to be gained rather than the specific goal itself. Goals are really a means to an end rather than the end itself and if your goal does become the end itself, what happens when you've achieved it? Why do you want it?

Some entrepreneurs dream of starting a company and growing it for a number of years with a view to floating on the stock market and capital-ising on the increased share value. When this is the 'end in mind' it can have a detrimental effect on employees. In one company, such was the focus on the stock market offer that it was the only goal people talked about. Then the day of their market listing came, shares were sold, some people made a handsome profit, and a big vacuum soon followed. There was nothing to go for any more that was half as exciting as the stock market listing. As for the entrepreneur, well he went on to make even more money and create more vacuums for other people elsewhere. ▶

> ▶On the other hand, more successful business leaders may be equally aware of the higher outcomes associated with success, such as providing jobs and security for people, creating a great place to work or offering the best products and services to their customers.

EXERCISE Link your goal to a higher purpose

1 Choose a goal that you have in mind and write it down.

2 Now ask yourself the following questions several times, or better, get a friend to ask you:

   – 'Why do I want this goal?'

   – 'What will it give me or do for me?'

3 When you get a really compelling reason accompanied by a positive feeling, write it down.

Have you ever wished you could see into the future and know the outcome of a course of action before taking it? Wouldn't it be useful to have the benefit of hindsight before you even start? Allowing your imagination to do just that is a powerful way of setting goals, creating the desire and motivation to make them happen and knowing what you need to do along the way.

MOUNTAIN

"High in the sky there can be seen towering a tall mountain. Were one but to wish to climb it, a path of ascent exists."   Japanese Waka poetry

Denise was visiting South Africa and wanted to take in the spectacular views of Cape Town from the top of Table Mountain. From the ground, the mountain appeared huge and extremely steep, to the point of being almost vertical, and the only way to the top seemed to be via cable car. Once at the top, however, as she looked down, she noticed that certain aspects of the mountain were a lot less steep, that some of the barriers to climbing now appeared much smaller, and she was also able to see all the various routes to the top which hadn't been visible from the ground.

When setting goals, starting with the end in mind helps you see where you want to get to and gain that mountain-top view before you begin, enabling you to see possibilities and choices rather than having a restricted view obscured by obstacles and limitations, and it can even make the mountain appear much smaller!

The following exercise is designed to help you start with the end in mind, know what you want to achieve, and have a clear understanding of the steps to take along the way. It uses the concept of physical space to help you associate with your goal. It will also help you to identify and remove any blocks and open up more possible routes to success. It brings the goal closer and strengthens your belief that it is possible.

EXERCISE Timeline

1 Think of a goal that you want to achieve.

2 Visualise a line across the floor and place a marker at the nearest end to represent 'now'.

3 Place a second marker at the far end to represent the moment in the future when you achieve your goal.

4 Standing on 'now', imagine that you have achieved this goal and create a vivid image, noticing all that you see, hear and feel now that you have it, and project this image onto the future end of your line.

5 Next, walk along the line to the point where you have achieved your goal. State in the present tense what you have now, and really experience how it feels. Act it out, or adopt a posture to represent success.

6 Now walk a few steps further into the future, beyond the point where you have achieved your goal, turn around and look back along the line.

7 As you look back, ask yourself, 'What did I have to do?' and 'What has to have happened in order for me to achieve this goal?' Get a mental image of each of the steps or tasks.

8 Walk back through each stage on the timeline, noticing all that you see, hear and feel. Imagine being there.

9 Now ask yourself, 'What happened just before this?', then walk to the spot just before that one. Continue until you arrive back at 'now'.

10 Capture all your thoughts and ideas.

EXERCISE Reverse storyboard

This is a similar exercise to Timeline, except that you will be creating a story-board of the path to your goal, a bit like a strip cartoon but in reverse. You will begin by drawing and describing an image of what it will be like when you have successfully achieved your goal. The significance of the image is to keep the imagination engaged at this stage and allow the widest possible thinking to occur at each individual step in the process.

1 Spend some time imagining what it will be like when you have achieved your goal. See your environment and the people in it. Hear what people are saying to you and to each other. Ask a friend to help you with this future exploration.

2 Create a picture or some form of image to represent the essence of your projected thoughts.

3 Write a statement (in the present tense) describing this image of your goal. For instance, 'I now have a rewarding and fulfilling job...'

4 Set a date for achievement and write that alongside the image.

5 Now, record all the events and activities that will need to have happened for you to have succeeded at your goal, and include a timescale for each one. You are working backwards from the achieved goal to the present day, so you will be working from right to left. Cut out each image, glue it to a large piece of card and hang it on the wall. When you have completed the story-board, you will be able to use the timescales to help create a more detailed plan in the next stage.

By creating each frame in the storyboard you will be encouraged to consider the key dynamics and requirements of that stage in your overall plan. You are likely to identify some things that may not have occurred to you until now. Remember to stay in a creative state of mind – which means no judgement or evaluation!

See the diagram below for a simple version of a reverse storyboard. In this example, the goal is quite complex, so you could take each individual frame and create another reverse storyboard of that stage. It all depends on how big or complex your goal is. Regardless of the size, each frame in the storyboard will become a sub-goal. When you create the storyboard, make the images as motivating as possible. You could even cut out pictures from magazines rather than draw or paint them yourself. The more fun you have doing this, the more creative you will be.

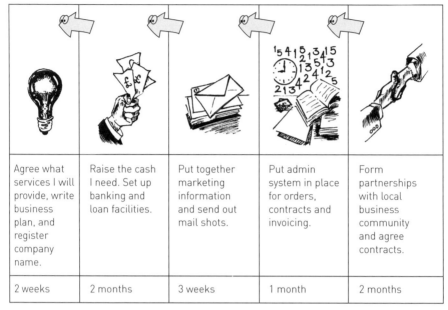

Agree what services I will provide, write business plan, and register company name.	Raise the cash I need. Set up banking and loan facilities.	Put together marketing information and send out mail shots.	Put admin system in place for orders, contracts and invoicing.	Form partnerships with local business community and agree contracts.
2 weeks	2 months	3 weeks	1 month	2 months

Reverse storyboard for setting up a contracted services business

This strategy can be used for any type of goal, from creating a business plan to learning to play the saxophone. Later we will show you how to work with your storyboard and progress through the Realist and Critic stages.

Strategies for the Realist

Imagine a plane flying on a journey from A to Z. The pilot knows the destination, keys the coordinates into the on-board computer and the automatic pilot takes over. During the flight, changes in wind speed and direction and other weather patterns begin to take the plane off course. Because of the on-board computer, the plane is able to recognise this and make the necessary adjustments to get back on track. For up to 80 per cent of the journey the plane may

be off course. However, because the final destination is known in advance and programmed into its computer, it succeeds in reaching its target.

Knowing what you want and focusing attention in that direction enables you to reach your goal and not get caught up in obstacles along the way. It also helps you recognise when you are going off track and need to make some fine adjustments. Now you can take a pragmatic look at each frame in your storyboard and begin to put some clear actions in place.

Setting robust outcomes

The type of goal you have chosen may consist of one or more separate sub-goals, or it may simply have one single step. Whatever you have chosen, you will want to think carefully about the outcomes and put the measures and resources in place to make sure you achieve them. The acronym PRIEST will help to make your outcomes as robust as they can possibly be.

P *Positively stated outcome*

The more specific you can be in stating what you want to achieve, and the more compelling you make it, the more chance you will have of actually achieving it. For the marketing example this might be described as follows:

'To create marketing materials that will motivate people to respond and get in touch with me, and to build a mailing list of over 10,000 names,

> Whatever you have chosen, you will want to
> think carefully about the outcomes and put the
> measures and resources in place to make sure
> you achieve them.

within the city central postcode areas, of companies which are likely to benefit from using my service.'

R *Resources required*

This includes both internal resources such as confidence, self-belief, motivation, knowledge, skills and mindset, and external resources of money, people, information and equipment. In our example this might include knowledge of marketing and skills in designing marketing materials, or other people who might provide these services. You would also need the money to pay for all of this, plus confidence to see it all through; the perseverance and concentration to work with the small details of a mailing list; the ability to articulate your message so that prospects will be motivated to contact you; and the information to know which companies to target.

I *Initiate and maintain the goal by yourself*

This is a key element in controlling what happens, and serves as a reminder that the more you allow other people to make important decisions that impact you, the less control you will have over achieving your outcome. The degree by which you involve others and delegate to them can be decided only by you and the confidence you have in their abilities and motivation to help you achieve your goal. There is an art to delegation where you remain in control using frequent performance reviews which are agreed at the outset. You can minimise the risk that comes with involving other people by asking yourself this question before handing over crucial decisions or actions: 'What's the personal risk to me if it doesn't happen?' Let's apply this to our example.

Let's say you ask a marketing company to come up with three designs for your materials and they have agreed to do this by the end of June, so leaving three weeks to produce and deliver the goods. Imagine that the day after you have given the marketing brief the company gets an angry call from one of its biggest clients. As a consequence they stop work on smaller clients' projects – including yours – to concentrate on their immediate problem. It's a survival response and it happens often in lots of companies. So now they have less time to complete and deliver your project. The next thing to happen is someone goes off sick and they lose another three days from your project. Time is slipping away and you, the client, don't even know it is happening.

If you trust people to do what they have agreed, you may be let down on occasion. This doesn't mean that other people intend to let you down; it's just that, like you, they are juggling lots of other priorities. So, in this case it would be advisable to get the company's agreement on exactly when they will commence work, and build in some check-points to review their progress. If they fail to deliver on time, it is you who learns the lesson, not the company.

E *Ecological impact on other people and situations*

Take a wide view of your goal and consider how it might affect all aspects of your life. You do not exist in a vacuum, so what impact will the work of achieving your goal have on other people and situations that connect with your life? Consider family, friends, environment, activities, travelling, lifestyle and other plans. In our example, you may have to take over a part of your house for an office from which to create and launch your marketing plans. How will this affect other people living in the house? How will it affect you? Will you be able to break off from work and relax, or will the home office be a constant reminder of work to be done? How much time will this take, and how will your relationships and social life be affected? Have you considered what life will be like in these very different circumstances?

S *Sensory-based evidence with which to measure success*

How will you know when you have successfully achieved your goal or any one of your sub-goals? Having a warm feeling is great for desire and motivation, but if you want to keep it you had better know how to measure your efforts. In the example, you might decide that a measure of success is 10 per cent returns on marketing, with 5 per cent conversion to service contracts, which will give you \$X,XXX of income. For the overall goal you may decide to measure your success by quantitative and qualitative measures. Whichever you choose, you just need to make sure that visible and/or auditory evidence exists in the plan with which you can measure your progress.

T *Time phased*

You will want to put a timescale on certain achievements. By when do you want to have completed each stage? This is simply a matter of estimating how much time will be required to achieve your goal or each sub-goal. Be realistic here. Some things take much longer than you think, and if you associate fully with each frame in your storyboard you will identify all the tasks that need to be done. The work you do here will be used to create a project plan containing every individual task to be completed.

OK. Now it's time to prepare a plan.

Plan to succeed

Now that you know all the steps involved in reaching your goal you're ready to create a plan to include all the 'what, where, when, how and who' answers. You are moving closer to the detail, and this is the easy part. Don't start to think you need a fancy planner or project management system; these often serve as a distraction to your goal. If you have one that works for you, fine, continue using it. If you don't, then find the simplest system possible. Many successful entrepreneurs have the simplest of systems. Richard Branson, head of the Virgin empire, has one notebook that he carries everywhere and which he uses to help run

If the work you are doing is meaningful for you, planning will be much easier. You will instinctively remember the important tasks.

his very diverse range of businesses. If the work you are doing is meaningful for you, planning will be much easier. You will instinctively remember the important tasks.

Just take each of your sub-goals or frames in your storyboard and brainstorm to identify all the individual tasks that must be done to achieve your outcome. We emphasise brainstorm because it is useful to maintain an aspect of creativity throughout the Realist stage. In this way you are more likely to identify all the tasks required. As you do this, make sure you adopt a Realist state of mind and look for the things that 'in reality' are likely to be needed to happen. The following exercise will help you to get your tasks organised.

EXERCISE Plan your success

1 Begin by using a mind map to record the tasks to be done.[2] When you have identified them all, begin to cluster them into categories of tasks that go together. As you do this, imagine being there, doing the tasks. Have a sense of reality about each task.

2 Next, identify the tasks that can be started first.

3 Identify tasks that can be started after the first ones are completed, and continue this process until all tasks have been given a place in the sequence.

4 Now you can begin to list the tasks in sequence. You have completed the 'what' part of the process.

5 Next to each task attach the 'when, by whom, where and how' information relevant to your goal.

2 The *Mind Map Book* by Tony and Barry Buzan, Dutton, 1996.

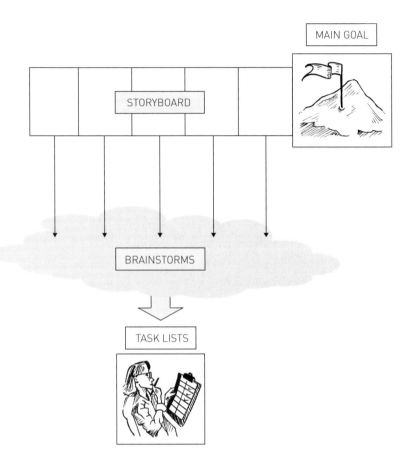

Now you have a plan of action, it's time to focus on the details.

Strategies for the Critic

It's now time to put on the Critic's hat and look for all the things that could possibly go wrong. Get into the Critic state of mind and focus on strengthening your plan. Take each sub-goal and review the brainstormed list and the task list. It is advisable – indeed it is particularly important at this stage – to ask for help from

other people since you will be very close to your plans by now and may be somewhat blinkered to unforeseen weaknesses. Choose people who have no idea about what you are doing. You will find that they ask the simplest questions that expose important aspects of your thinking. Also choose other people who have experience of what you are doing. You can benefit from their perspectives and knowledge. Ask them to pull no punches and make sure they know that their input is valuable to you.

Role-play

Set up a role-play scenario where you are acting the various scenes involved with your goal. Ask friends or colleagues to play clients and act out customer meetings. Set up role-plays to test your logic, thinking and ability to articulate your message to other people you want to influence. Ask your colleagues to give you feedback on what works and what can be improved. Are they convinced you're on a winning track?

What could you lose?

Take each separate activity and look for any possible hidden risks and consider the worst possible scenarios of any inherent risks. Hidden risks are usually the ones that appear from nowhere and really bite you hard on the rear end. Inherent risks are ones that are accepted as part of the assessed risk of achieving the goal. In our marketing example you might recognise an inherent risk in the marketing effort of getting little or no response, so you might have a built-in contingency to kick in an alternative strategy of marketing via business seminars. However, what if the service contract business should suddenly change radically, causing companies to adopt a sophisticated government standard? Perhaps an unlikely situation, but it is the most unlikely ones that will catch you out.

Having well thought-through contingencies is all part of the Critic process, and while the ideal is to cover all eventualities, it is highly

unlikely that you will. Go with what is reasonably possible with the resources you have and the rest you can keep an eye on.

Alternative perspectives

This technique will help you to take an objective view of what you are about to do. It uses visualisation to step out of your shoes and adopt the perspectives of other people you will be coming into contact with during your goal journey. You can use this for each sub-goal in your storyboard, or for any part of your plan. It can be very effective for situations where you are considering the important interactions you will be having with other people, such as business partners, bank managers, suppliers and prospective clients. Think of it as a role-play where you are sequentially acting out three different roles: 1) yourself, 2) another person and 3) an observer watching the interaction between 1 and 2.

EXERCISE Gaining perspective

1 Mark two locations on the floor, about 6ft apart, or use different chairs. Choose a significant other person who will play a part in you achieving your goal and become that person as you stand at one of the marked locations.

2 On the other marked spot project an image of yourself doing what it will take to achieve your goal. Project a movie of events unfolding and include the words you think the other person might say. What questions might they have for you? What might their concerns be? What are their priorities?

3 As the significant person, concentrate on the image of 'you' that you are projecting onto the other location and consider what it will be like interacting with you. Think about how the two of you will communicate. Ask questions about motivation, values and beliefs.

4 Now add a third marked location and stand on that as an observer. Watch yourself and the significant other person as they are interacting. Can you draw any new insights from the movie you project from this perspective?

In addition to the very specific techniques and strategies we have included here, remember to discuss your plans with other people, and ask lots of questions. Gather as much information as you possibly can.

The following quote from Bertrand Russell is of a metaphor he used to describe his strategy for writing books:

"The nearest analogy is first walking all over a mountain in a mist, until every path and ridge and valley is separately familiar, and then, from a distance, seeing the mountain whole and in bright sunshine."

Additional resources are available from the **Quadrant1.com** website. Go to **www.quadrant1.com**, click on know-how and select the title you want.

- Goal setting
- Stakeholder analysis
- Time.

8

Staying on track

❝The person with a fixed goal, a clear picture of his desire, or an ideal always before him, causes it, through repetition, to be buried deeply in his subconscious mind and is thus enabled, thanks to its generative and sustaining power, to realise his goal in a minimum of time and with a minimum of physical effort. Just pursue the thought unceasingly. Step by step you will achieve realisation, for all your faculties and powers become directed to that end.❞   Claude M. Bristol

Your dreams, desires and goals are like a compass in your heart guiding you on your journey and letting you focus 100 per cent of your conscious attention on each single moment. So now that you've set your goal, you're clear about what you want and you have a plan, it's time for action. Your goals won't materialise by themselves – well, not usually! The key to success from here on is taking action, staying focused and maintaining momentum. You may know what it's like to set out with lots of good intentions and then not get to the finish. So to make sure that you really do succeed in beating your goals, here are some tips to keep you on the path to success and to make sure your goals continue to be what you want them to be.

Making it happen or letting it happen

❝When you are following your higher will there is a balance between being carried by the current and feeling that you are using your own will to create results.❞   Sanaya Roman

**The key to success from here on is taking action,
staying focused and maintaining momentum.**

How much effort do you need to invest in achieving your goals? Some people think it's got to be hard work all the way, while others believe that if you have to struggle then you're on the wrong path and not using your energy effectively.

You may remember occasions in the past when you felt you were fighting a losing battle and just weren't making progress. There may have been other times when things just seemed to happen easily and effortlessly. Perhaps it was when you were hitting a tennis ball, reading a novel or working out at the gym. If you take no action towards achieving your goals and wait for fate to decide, the chances are you won't achieve what you want. And when you are struggling, pushing and working hard and still not achieving results, maybe you're not being true to yourself or focusing your energy in the most effective way.

There is a balance to be found between letting the current take you and steering your own course. When what you're doing is working, that's great, and when it isn't – it's time to do something else! Don't fight against the current. Use your energy wisely.

Andy, wanted to set up a rickshaw business in the city centre where he lived. Everything was flowing well until the time came to agree the operational conditions with the city council. Unforeseen red tape slowed down the business plans and this made Andy very frustrated. His response was to get angry and make unreasonable demands to try to push through a decision. The more he pushed, the longer the council took. Eventually he ran out of money and the idea never got off the ground. In hindsight, rather than push the way he did, Andy might have put his energy else- ▶

▶where to give his idea the best chance of working. For example, he might have been more civil and patient with the council, while at the same time exploring other town and city centres looking for suitable alternative locations to launch the service.

EXERCISE Creating a natural energy flow

● Think of a time when you felt as though you were putting in lots of effort and yet were still struggling to make progress. What was the outcome? How did it feel? Where was your focus of attention? How would you like it to have been different?

● Now think of a time when you achieved something almost effortlessly and easily. What was the outcome? How did it feel? Where was your focus of attention? What was different?

● Now think of a current goal. Notice what comes easily and anything that feels more like a struggle. What options do you have for making it easier, working smarter, involving others? How else can you achieve your higher goal?

Intuition

In a *Harvard Business Review* article in February 2001, Alden M. Hayashi describes how many successful business executives make crucial decisions 'by relying on their intuitive skills'.[1] Have you ever just had a 'hunch' that something was the right thing to do or that an idea was really good? That's what we call 'intuition' and there is so much everyday evidence that only a fool would refute that it has a direct effect on our lives.

---

1 'When to trust your gut' by Alden M. Hayashi, Harvard Business Review, February 2001.

Michael has experienced repeated success at setting up in business and making money. In fact, he's one of those people who just can't help it. When asked how he goes about achieving his goals he admits that earning the money wasn't actually the goal. His goal was more to do with achieving business success and yet he doesn't know precisely how he achieves it. In his words, he 'just does it'. When asked about his success, Michael uses words like 'following an unturnable current', 'instinct is everything', 'trust your instinct', 'do what feels right', 'listen to the signs', 'have the confidence and courage to trust yourself'.

Intuition is that state or process of knowing something that you didn't think you knew and is often connected with feelings, hence the reason why people talk about having a 'gut feeling', or having an 'instinct'. Intuition is often described as a deep unconscious intelligence or higher consciousness which seems to give us signals generated from the creative part of our mind. In fact, the word 'intuition' could be written as 'inner tuition', or deep learning. We lead such busy lives, and our senses take in much more information than we can deal with in our conscious or 'alert' state. If we tried to remember every detail of each day, we would probably blow a fuse. The unconscious or creative part of our mind seems to be very good at recognising patterns from all our previous experiences, and it may be that intuition is the unconscious mind making a connection between something in the alert state and a pattern of information previously stored and processed by the unconscious mind. Or it may be that we pick up messages from an even higher level of consciousness. Whatever is going on, it's certainly worth tuning in to these inner signals, as your intuition works for your personal benefit and has your best interests in mind.

When you follow your intuition you are on the right path and what you're doing feels right. It will give you a signal if the goal you have chosen is not going to be good for you. Using your intuition is helpful when you have a decision to make and there is insufficient information available to help you decide logically, or so much information that it becomes overwhelming. It is, of course, important to balance your intuition with action, patience and trust in order to carry out your ideas and turn them into reality.

EXERCISE Developing your intuitive power

1 Think about a situation you have yet to decide on and for which you have very little information.

2 Relax and tell yourself that your intuition has the answer. Breathe deeply and calmly and spend a few minutes thinking about your situation.

3 Take a walk outside and allow your eyes to rest upon objects as they come into your view. Choose one object to help you interpret your intuition. The object you choose can be any size or shape, and it may just seem like the right object for this purpose.

4 Consider the object's function and relate that to your situation. What does it tell you?

5 Next, consider the object's form and relate that to your situation. What does it tell you?

Tips for developing your intuition

- Tune into your intuition and learn to recognise the feelings it uses to communicate with you.

- Learn to trust your intuition.

- Find ways of relaxing and accessing your intuition.

- Notice any patterns in your life that your unconscious mind is alerting you to.

- Meditate, listen to music, exercise, play, and use objects as metaphors.

- Recognise the physical signals when you know you have a good idea.

- Let your deeper wisdom or inner compass guide you.

- Do what 'feels right' rather than struggle.

- Check – is it your intuition or an emotion such as fear or anger?

- Gather feedback from others.

- Make intuitive decisions and be prepared to make adjustments.

- When you feel uneasy, check out your feelings using rational questions about your situation. Ask, 'What don't I know about this situation?'

The future begins now

"The only way to deal with the future is to function efficiently in the now."

Gita Bellin

When you focus too much on your future goal and pay little attention to what's happening in the present, you may miss opportunities, get distracted, overlook feedback and not enjoy the journey. By setting a goal in the future you are combining intent with your dream and desire, and when you balance this with present-moment awareness you have a very powerful combination.

Before a tennis match or competition, players will focus on the outcome they want – the end in mind. During the match, successful players focus on one point and one shot at a time, avoiding distractions and doing exactly what's required at that moment. And with each point they win they know that they are one step closer to achieving their higher goal of winning the match and even the tournament.

This is what Mihaly Csikszentmihalyi calls 'flow'.[2] In moments of optimal performance when you are completely engrossed in an activity, time seems to stand still and you achieve your goal using the skills you have. When a person experiences 'flow' Csikszentmihalyi suggests that certain conditions exist:

1   Clear and challenging goals that require skills and which originate from within the individual.

2   Being fully immersed in the activity.

3   Receiving feedback.

4   Paying attention to what is happening in the moment.

5   Having a sense of being in control.

6   Enjoying the immediate experience.

Having a clear goal and being aware of what's happening right now will enable you to act on feedback, make good choices, adjust as necessary and use your energy in the most effective way. Focusing on one step at a time enables you to progress as each achievement takes you closer to your higher goal.

Imagine delivering a presentation to a large audience and at the same time thinking about something you missed in your introduction or the next meeting you're due to attend. When you don't pay full attention you will appear distracted, even disconnected from your audience, and the power behind your message will be lost. Your presentation will have far more impact and you will have much greater presence when you focus on where you are right now and connect with your audience.

---

2 *Flow – the Psychology of Happiness* by Mihaly Csikszentmihalyi, Rider, 1992.

 **Gaining control over your thinking, your attention and your reactions to external events will help you achieve your goals.**

In our work we frequently meet people who tell us that they are unable to turn off their mind or inner voice. In just about every case we find that the person is trying to hold on to too many thoughts at one time and is less able to focus on what they are doing in the present. At the extreme this can begin to create stress and other symptoms. Learning to relax and manage your energy is a way of coping with this and an increasing number of people are now taking up regular exercise such as tai chi, qigong or yoga to help balance their energy and regain their health. Gaining control over your thinking, your attention and your reactions to external events will help you achieve your goals.

Many of our coaching clients are very capable and experienced people who know how to achieve goals, but their high stress levels are reducing their capacity to fix attention on one thing at a time and put their full attention to the strategic concepts they are working on. Often the solution is not more thinking, rather we help them learn to slow down their minds and rebalance their mind/body energy so they can attain a natural flow to their work and their life.

EXERCISE	Will you 'flow' with your goal?

Here are some questions to check how much the goal you have chosen to pursue will provide the conditions for you to experience the state of flow.

1 Is your goal something you created?

2 As you think about your goal does it appear to be something you connect with strongly, or is it more connected with other people and/or situations in your environment?

3   What feedback will help to keep you on track? How frequently will it be available to you?

4   Will your goal require you to use existing skills and learn new ones?

5   How much of a challenge will your goal be for you personally?

6   To what degree will you enjoy the activities you will be doing in pursuit of your goal?

7   Are you able to concentrate fully on one task without being distracted?

8   To what degree do you feel in control of things?

9   How easy is it for you to relax and enjoy other activities unconnected with your goal?

Holding on or letting go

"Life is a series of natural and spontaneous changes. Don't resist them – that only creates sorrow. Let reality be reality. Let things flow naturally forward in whatever way they like."   Lao-Tse

Sometimes the path to your goal isn't a direct one. Much like the plane flying from A to Z, there may be obstacles to overcome and you may find you need to make some changes as you go. If you stick too rigidly to your plan and take no account of changing circumstances, you might jeopardise your success.

Dan runs a successful company, which is growing rapidly, and part of the strategy for growth involves acquiring other companies. Dan knows, as well as anyone, that some of these deals will prove successful and others might not. If he were to become too attached to one particular deal and it fell through, that might be seen as failure and discourage him from pursuing his mission. Instead, by focusing on the purpose, the dream and the vision for the company, he remains open to other opportunities and discovering even better ones.

Often we hold on too tightly to a specific goal or to our plans and decisions, and when we lack flexibility and the plan doesn't work out, we don't get to realise our dreams. How often do you get caught up with wanting people to do things exactly as you would do them? This desire for something to be precisely as you imagine, combined with a reluctance to let go, is often one of the things that prevents people from working with others and achieving what they want. If you keep too tight a grasp on the reins you might lose sight of what's most important.

"It's critical that you focus on the result and not get attached to any particular process for achieving the result." Joseph Jaworski

In his book entitled *Synchronicity: The Inner Path of Leadership*, Joseph Jaworski describes what happened at a time when his successful business hit difficulties.[3] He realised that he had reverted to focusing rigidly on the business plan instead of focusing on the vision they had intended, and that this was the exact opposite of what he had done during their most successful phase when he had been focusing on the dream, remaining highly flexible, going with the flow of things, taking one day at a time and listening for guidance about the next step.

At a time of crisis he had battened down the hatches and reverted to traditional ways of operating, and they weren't working. Fortunately, he was able to recognise what was happening in time and change his approach.

So sometimes it's helpful to relax your need for the outcome or the process to be exactly how you imagine and allow yourself to be more open and flexible. This way of thinking frees you from past limitations

3 Synchronicity: *The Inner Path to Leadership* by Joseph Jaworski, Berrett-Koehler Publishers, San Francisco, 1996.

and being restricted by what you already know, and creates space for new and even better possibilities. When you do encounter obstacles, recognise how these can help you to learn and grow stronger. You might even find on occasions that not achieving one goal leads you to something even better.

"There is no such thing as a problem without a gift for you in its hands. You seek problems because you need their gifts." Richard Bach

EXERCISE Working with boundaries

1 Select a goal.

2 Identify which aspects of the goal or the process are fixed, i.e. where there is no scope for change or variance.

3 Identify those aspects where there is scope for variance.

4 Decide where the boundaries are.

5 Get into a playful, creative state and ask yourself:

  − 'What other options do I have?'

  − 'Where else could this lead?'

  − 'What could happen if I let go of this problem?'

  − 'How might (another person) deal with this?'

  − 'How can I shift my thinking?'

Persistence and determination

"With increased inner strength it is possible to develop firm determination and with determination there is a greater chance of success, no matter what obstacles there may be." The Dalai Lama

Some people seem to achieve their goals against all odds, overcoming seemingly insurmountable obstacles and setbacks along the way. They say that when the going gets tough, the tough get going, and there will be times that desire and motivation alone are not enough. Sometimes you will require persistence and dogged determination.

Walt Disney was once fired by a newspaper editor for a lack of ideas, and he was turned down by over 300 banks before being given the finance to build his theme park.

Thomas Edison was told by his teachers that he was too stupid to learn anything, and he had numerous failures before he finally invented the light bulb.

You may know some people who have lots of determination to overcome obstacles and they may be seen as having strong personal motivation, yet most of us at some time will experience low motivation to complete a task. There may be times where no matter how important your goals are, you need to do things that you don't always enjoy.

Rose is a successful sales manager. As with any job, there are aspects that she likes less than others and yet she knows they need to be done. Recently she was telling us how the company was under pressure to generate more business and that her team were reluctant to cold-call potential customers because they didn't like doing it. Her response was that, whether she likes it or not, she will persevere and get on with it because it needs to be done. This could explain how Rose succeeds where others do not.

To really beat your goals you must remain committed and determined to do whatever it takes, even though some tasks you will enjoy more than others.

If you give up at the first sign of difficulty you won't achieve what you set out to do. To really beat your goals you must remain committed and determined to do whatever it takes, even though some tasks you will enjoy more than others. When it comes to enjoyment it's the overall journey that matters. You should be able to take on some tasks that have little immediate fulfilment, as long as the goal is personally worthy, motivating and valuable.

❝Unless you try to do something beyond what you have already mastered, you will never grow.❞
Ralph Waldo Emerson

EXERCISE Test your willpower and determination to succeed

For each of the statements below score as follows:

5 if True most of the time.

3 if True some of the time and False at other times.

1 if False most of the time.

	1	3	5
I am self-disciplined			
I rarely procrastinate			
I know what I want			
I am willing to work hard to get it			
I am not easily distracted			

	1	3	5
I persist in doing tasks I don't enjoy			
I prefer to take direct action than to think and plan			
I am not easily put off by obstacles			
I don't waste time focusing on the problems and things that could go wrong			
I am sometimes described as stubborn			
When I decide to do something I stick at it			
My willpower is rock solid			
I never blame others when things go wrong			

Scoring the exercise

65 is the highest score and suggests you are a very determined individual. The statements where you have scored either a 3 or a 1 indicate where you are able to make progress in the determination stakes – if you are determined enough to make the necessary changes, that is.

For those occasional times when your motivation may be low or when you are faced with obstacles, your will and determination will help you through. Use the following tips to create the determination to help you beat your goals.

- **Purpose and desire**

  Check that you have a higher purpose or outcome that is meaningful and worthwhile, and focus on the end goal. Visualise the moment you succeed and answer the question: What purpose in my life am I fulfilling?

- **Take one step at a time**

  Doing something is better than doing nothing. Take actions that carry you closer to your goal. Just do something.

- **Build on what you already have**

  Recognise the value of what you have done so far and notice how far you've come, not just how far you still have to go.

- **State of mind**

  Train your mind to remember those occasions when you did persevere and were successful. Get into a positive state of mind and reframe any negative thoughts into positive, empowering thoughts.

- **Management**

  Have a clear plan and manage your time. Allow for a degree of flexibility and allocate time for distractions and rewards after you've completed certain tasks.

- **Positive thoughts**

  Focus on solutions rather than problems and concentrate on what you *can* do, not what you *can't*.

- **Belief**

  Believe that it's possible, that you will beat your goals, and trust yourself.

- **Habits**

  Develop good habits that move you forward (see New habit generator exercise below).

- JUST DO IT ... The NIKE slogan. How much could you have done in the time you've spent thinking about it?

If you have recognised any new habits you want to develop, they can be easily learned, and one sure-fire way is by repetition. *If 'bad' habits are easily picked up then 'good' habits can be created too.* New habits can take 2–4 weeks to condition, so to make sure that you stay the course use our 'New habit generator' worksheet to plan the new habit into each day and condition yourself for success.

EXERCISE New habit generator

This worksheet is designed for anyone finding it hard to muster enough discipline to make goals a reality. It is a simple checklist system based on the premise that if you repeat a behaviour for 30 days it will become a habit. The worksheet is in two parts.

Part 1 – Getting focused

Think about the following four part-statements carefully and complete each one in the adjoining box. This will serve as a reminder for the duration of the exercise.

The things I value most in life are ...

The goals I have set myself are ...

New habits I want to develop are ...

My immediate goal-related activities are ...

Part 2 – The 30-day plan

Begin by bringing your dream into your mind and internalising what it means for you at an intuitive level. Next, refer to the worksheet below and read your values. Remind yourself why this dream is so important to you and reaffirm your determination to beat your goals. Now list the main goal-related tasks that are important for you to do consistently each day, and for which you want

to develop more effective habits. For example, you might decide that three goal-related tasks are:

1 networking

2 telesales

3 research.

You may want to be more consistent and habitual at telesales, so this would be something to do every day for 30 days. In this way it will become second nature to do so and you will be less likely to procrastinate or be distracted by other things. Just write it down and tick it off each day when you've done it. Finally, recall recent activities and plan your day by making a simple list of the tasks you intend to get done. Do this every day and you will soon have the habits you want.

	April											
Motivation and organisation	1	2	3	4	5	6	7	8	9	10	...	30
Internalise your dream	✔	✔										
Read your values	✔	✔										
Review goal and sub-goals	✔	✔										
Plan the day	✔	✔										
Goal-related actions												
1 Networking	✔	✔										
2 Telesales	✔	✔										
3 Research	✔	✔										
4 Health and energy	✔	✔										
5 Learn language												
6 Make new contacts	✔											▶

New habits	
1 Call at least three prospects	✔
2 Speak with a colleague	✔
3 Do my e-mail twice only	✔
4 Do 30 mins exercise	✔

Get some feedback

Once you've set your goals and have a plan there really shouldn't be any surprises. If you are focused on your goal and aware of what's happening in the present you will be constantly gathering information to show how you're progressing or what you need to change to stay on track. You might also notice new opportunities that can help you progress even more. Without feedback you might miss out on these or even find that the goal is no longer appropriate.

Feedback is available all the time if you look for it, so develop your external awareness and have your antennae out constantly. It may be a feeling you have, a reaction from someone, or some solid facts and information. You can also choose the sort of feedback that will be helpful, such as advice or suggestions, and proactively seek it out. For instance, you might ask someone to review a piece of work you've done or listen to you rehearse a presentation.

Even if you believe in yourself and your capabilities it is always a good idea to get some feedback. In fact, it could be downright suicidal not to.

 Feedback is available all the time if you look for it, so develop your external awareness and have your antennae out constantly.

Other people are rating your effectiveness. Beware of relying on internally generated feedback alone. It may feel good to you, but did it feel good to others? In any enterprise or social pursuit it is other people's judgement of you that will determine your degree of success, so if external feedback is not offered, you had better ask for it, or better – design a way of getting it systematically.

EXERCISE **Asking for what you want**

- Decide what you want, e.g. information, advice, suggestions, different perspectives.
- Choose whom to ask, e.g. friends, colleagues, experts, customers.
- Help them to give you what you want by asking specific questions.
- Thank them.
- Decide how to use it.
- Follow it up.

Measure progress

When you notice or receive feedback you want to make sure you make the most of it as all feedback is an opportunity to learn and is vital in helping you to beat your goals. When receiving feedback from other people, requested or otherwise, here are some tips to bear in mind.

- Keep an open mind.
- Listen carefully, evaluate later.
- Do not justify, make excuses or get defensive.
- Ask for clarification if it's unclear.
- Decide how to use it.

It can be easy to overlook or undervalue feedback. One way of capturing all the feedback you get, whether specific comments or just things you notice, is to record what you learn from it. Sometimes feedback highlights strengths and opportunities, and it can also make you aware of areas for development and obstacles to be overcome. Use the following table to record the opportunities you encounter and any obstacles that present themselves. For each opportunity decide how you will use it and for each obstacle use this book to help you overcome it and move on. Each stage will help you move nearer to your goal.

GOAL: launch new business offering			
Feedback	Opportunity	Obstacle	Action
Sue thinks I could be doing more with my idea.	What if she's right?		Call friends in the city to ask their views on expanding my service.
Bank manager is concerned at the amount of loan I have requested.		Bank will only loan 50 per cent of what I asked for.	Try other banks. Consider alternative approaches to business start-up.

Get support

Whether your goal is a joint goal with your team or a partner or a personal goal, you're not on your own. Seek out colleagues, friends, family and other contacts who can help you beat your goals. You might choose people who have knowledge, experience, contacts or resources to assist you. Build a contact list of all the people who can help you. Avoid judging their ability to help until you have approached them. Most people will either have some advice or will know someone else who may be able to help. If you keep your ideas and plans to yourself you will shut yourself off to the stimulation that comes from other people's ideas, knowledge, skills and contacts.

> In the world of networking and journalism, it is commonly accepted that it takes a maximum of only six people to connect any two people on the planet. So you can meet anyone you want if you find the people who can connect you.

Don't underestimate the power of networking in the pursuit of your goals. Most people you meet will want you to succeed and will be only too happy to be able to assist you with contacts and information. If you never ask, you will have to make do with what you can generate on your own. If this seems one-sided, remember that reciprocation is very powerful. Most people want to return a favour, and you would not expect to get everything you want for nothing, would you?

Helping others, with sincerity and without obligation, is the professional approach to networking. Rather than beginning with the things you want, start out by thinking of what you can do for others. Become a giver, a helper, a listener, a friend, and the things you want will come to you more easily. If you help others to be successful in some way, they will be more inclined to reciprocate and support your success.

If your goal involves developing your skills or overcoming personal limitations, consider using a personal coach to help you succeed. It is not so easy working through barriers on your own, and a coach can help you to break through the negative blocks you may be creating and move forward more confidently with drive and enthusiasm.

Integrate learning

"It's what you learn after you know it all that really counts."   John Wooden

This is possibly the most important ingredient for serial success. Unless you carry your learning forward you will make the same mistakes all over again. It is easy to think that because you have overcome an obstacle you will automatically adapt to a similar situation in the future. But this is rarely the case. You only have to look at business history to reveal how easily we repeat our mistakes.

Knowledge management is a key strategic goal for many commercial organisations today. It's basic premise is that knowledge exists in the experience of employees, and success comes from finding ways to share and use the collective knowledge and experience of all employees. Three basic symptoms of having a knowledge problem include:

- repeating the same mistakes;
- duplication of work;
- good ideas are not shared.

There are easy and hard ways of learning the lessons in life. The hard approach hits your pocket and your confidence. The easy approach hits your thinking, giving you time to develop a different approach.

"To strive with difficulties, and to conquer them, is the highest human felicity."   Samuel Johnson

All the barriers, problems, difficult decisions, puzzling people and red tape are challenges for you to overcome. Think of them as your teachers, helping you to become stronger and smarter – learning from your experience and building for the future. There will be some experiences you will want to avoid in the future and others you will want to repeat.

It's important therefore to make time to capture what you have learned and integrate it into your planning, your thinking and your behaviour. Review the path travelled, draw out the lessons, and integrate for the future.

EXERCISE	Review, learn and integrate

Consider a recent goal you have been pursuing and take some time to review it with a colleague or friend. Note down the things that worked well and those that you would have done differently with hindsight.

- What worked well?
- What could have been better?
- What will you do less of, more of, differently next time?

Celebrate success

Success can sometimes be followed by anti-climax. If you focus so much time, energy and effort on achieving one specific goal, what happens when you finally achieve it? Some people can be left wondering 'what now?' and feel a sense of loss, while others are already onto the next project.

It's important to acknowledge what you have achieved personally and what other contributors have achieved. After all, this is an important goal that you've been working towards, which supports even higher goals and values. You deserve to celebrate and recreate the positive feelings you had when you dreamed up this idea. By creating a really powerful, positive association with success this time you might build even more motivation to beat your next goal. Feelings of success build confidence and help to unleash further potential. If you suppress these feelings, either by ignoring your achievement or just not stopping to

**Feelings of success build confidence and help to
unleash further potential.**

acknowledge what you have managed to do, then success will cease to
be so enjoyable and may even slip by unnoticed. When you allow this
to continue over long periods it can have a detrimental effect on your
future success and energy levels. So be kind to yourself, treat yourself
and give yourself an energy boost to preserve your health and beat your
next goal too!

You are capable of anything you set your mind to, and the power of cel-
ebration can bring out more of your innate capability to succeed. Cele-
bration comes from the heart to stimulate your natural creative
resources. You might want to get together with your colleagues, buy
something special, take time out to relax, spend time with loved ones
or whatever else you enjoy. You owe it to yourself for all the work you
have put in to feel good whenever you achieve something. Regardless
of the size or type of goals you choose to aim for, feeling good about
yourself is what life is all about – and what else compares with making
your dreams come to life?

Additional resources are available from the **Quadrant1.com** website.
Go to **www.quadrant1.com**, click on know-how and select the title you want.

- Feedback – the fuel to power learning
- New habit generator
- Stress test.

Further resources to help you beat your goals

Available from Quadrant 1, leaders in coaching, learning and change.

- Contact David and Denise through the website at **www.quadrant1.com** where you will find a range of tips, tools and ideas to download from a growing database of practical resources.

- Subscribe to Know-How on the website and receive regular updates via e-mail to help you *be* and *do* your best.

- Organise a 'Beat Your Goals' workshop for your team or company.

- Ask us about one-to-one coaching and team coaching.

- Alignment – corporate initiatives to help you align people with a common purpose and give your business performance a real boost.

- Discover more about success in business through the following books:
    - *NLP Business Masterclass* by David Molden, Financial Times Prentice Hall, 2001.
    - *Realigning for Change* by David Molden and Jon Symes, Financial Times Pitman Publishing, 1999.
    - *Managing with the Power of NLP* by David Molden, Financial Times Prentice Hall, 1996.

- Discover how individuals, teams and corporations are putting these ideas to work by viewing the cases and articles in the media section of the website.

How to contact the authors

www.quadrant1.com

Tel: +44 (0) 1865 715 895
david@quadrant1.co.uk (David)
Tel: +44 (0) 20 8680 9154
denise@quadrant1.co.uk (Denise)